SHAPING THE COMMUNITY COLLEGE
LB2342.8 .S53 1993

A12644231001

DATE DUE

D0579420

Shaping the Community College

IMAGE

National Council

for Marketing and

Public Relations

in cooperation with

the Association of

Community College

Trustees

Edited by

Steven W. Jones, Ed.D.

Shaping the Community College Image

© 1993 by the National Council for Marketing and Public Relations
All rights reserved.
Published by NCMPR, 364 N. Wyndham Ave., Greeley, Colorado
80634.

NCMPR, an affiliate council of the American Association of
Community Colleges, is a professional organization of individuals
involved in marketing, communications and public relations at the
community, junior and technical colleges. NCMPR provides
professional development opportunities, advocates on behalf of the
profession and the institutions it serves, and recognizes professional
excellence.

Support for this publication was provided by the Association of
Community College Trustees (ACCT), 1740 N Street NW, Washington, D.C. 20036.

Library of Congress Catalog Number: 92-83906

ISBN: 0-9635800-1-9

Printed in the United States of America.

Shaping
the
Community
College

IMAGE

**National Council
for Marketing and
Public Relations**
in cooperation with
the Association of
Community College
Trustees

Edited by
Steven W. Jones, Ed.D.

CONTENTS

*T*o the trustees, administrators, public relations professionals—
and countless others—whose service and devotion
help shape the community college image.

*C*ommunity colleges are critical to the vitality of local communities and to that of the United States. They are the only educational institutions required to meet the diverse, constantly changing constituents' needs and workforce demands. Each year over 1,200 comprehensive two-year, community, technical and junior colleges enroll 10 million students in credit and non-credit courses. Each year these colleges, private and public, educate the equivalent of the combined population of New York City and the State of Wisconsin. In Wisconsin alone, one out of every eight adults is served annually by one of the 16 technical colleges. With that ratio, it is the rare adult in Wisconsin, who over a 10-year period, has not taken at least one course at a technical college. Other states have similar records. Yet, despite this high attendance, the image of community colleges remains unclear to much of the nation's populace.

As trustees, presidents and staff of community colleges, we have an obligation to ensure that the mission and contributions of our colleges are better understood. Historically, community colleges have served the disadvantaged who were denied access to other higher education institutions. Community colleges consistently have met the changing, diverse and most often competing demands of local constituents while ensuring educational quality and accountability. Why is it then, that the image of community colleges remains such a mystery? What role must we assume, as community college leaders, to communicate our exciting and responsive image?

Shaping the Community College Image assists us as practitioners and leaders in addressing these critical questions. Written by trustees, presidents and professionals in marketing and public relations, this book focuses on the strength of community colleges — our diversity — and strategies for shaping and communicating our vital local and national images. Throughout the book, we note the significance of community colleges in the national and international workforce. We examine what marketing is and what it is not. We discover the value of research and identification of market segmentation. We revisit basic marketing principles and examine the "big picture." We learn that as trustees and CEOs we have important roles to play in the development, enhancement and communication of our colleges' images. We realize that this task is too vital to be left in the hands of only a few college employees. We learn how, through work teams and community collaboration, we can maximize our marketing resources. We gain perspective on the pressures and conflicting demands on our institutions. And lastly, we come to appreciate more fully the distinction of our individual institutions and our unique value to our nation.

This book is a basic tool for all of us in the community college movement. Its thought-provoking language provides a vehicle for reflection on strategies to assist the nation in taking the confusion and mystery out of the community college image.

Our work is too important to be left unheralded. Now is the time for us to use the tools of effective research and marketing to ensure that our message — the value of community college outcomes — is clearly heard in every town, village and state. Nationally, we must loudly proclaim the significance of our work in preserving and enhancing the vitality of the United States. As other countries, like Denmark, England, and the Netherlands turn to our community college model for enhancing their educational systems and national productivity, we must reaffirm the strength and significance of our work.

As we collectively shape the community college image, let our voices and the accomplishments of our students proclaim the value of our 1,200 public and private community colleges.

Beverly Simone, Chair
Board of Directors
American Association of Community Colleges
President, Madison Area Technical College

EDITOR'S ACKNOWLEDGEMENTS

To travel hopefully is a better thing than to arrive.

--Robert Louis Stevenson

*F*or nearly two decades, I have traveled hopefully in my journey as an advocate for the community college. That journey has brought me insights as a community college student, faculty member, program director, department head, dean, vice president, and now as a president who works with a board of trustees.

At one point along that pilgrimage, was the challenge to serve as a community college public relations and marketing director. That experience prepared me well for a presidency, because a president is without question a college's chief public relations officer. And yet, it made me keenly aware of one of the great ironies of our profession.

Those of us who have invested our professional lives advancing the community college are often distressed to realize that while we may fully understand the significance of our colleges, so many who can help us advance them have a very distorted perspective of our colleges. A uniquely American institution, the community college has been a part of American higher education for almost a century. Yet, it remains an enigma to most opinion leaders and policy makers, many of whom relate almost exclusively to higher education through the model of the European university.

Caught up in one activity trap or another, I had failed to ponder the implications of that fact until a cherished friend sent me a discarded volume from a school library. The first chapter of that book, published in 1968, was entitled, "What in the World is a

Community College?" It is a question that we, as community leaders, still face today, a quarter of a century later. It made me realize that the time has come to forge a national community college image.

Through discussions with my friends and colleagues, Beverly Simone, AACC board chair, and Steve Lestarjette, NCMPR president, the framework for this book was constructed. The concept was embraced by visionaries within the Association of Community College Trustees (ACCT) and the National Council for Marketing and Public Relations (NCMPR). After months of planning, writing, editing, and production, the book is finally finished — but the challenges it presents have only begun.

This book is dedicated to the thousands of people who have devoted their careers to advance and promote the American community college. It is written for those who lead those colleges, presidents and trustees, and for those who contribute to the movement by serving as critical linking pins to their college's external constituencies.

The book is a collective effort of trustees, CEOs, public information officers, and dozens of community college colleagues and advisors. While they cannot all be acknowledged for their contributions, there are those who served as catalysts to this team project who deserve special recognition.

Without the support of Ray Taylor and Sally Hutchins from ACCT, this book would have never been possible. Once its need was established, the NCMPR Editorial Board provided invaluable guidance on content and prospective authors. Those board members include: Bob Burdick from Johnson County Community College, Walt Gallacher from Colorado Mountain College, Lucy Kubiszyn of Shelton State Community College, and Richard Petrizzo from the College of DuPage.

Other contributors to the project include Marlene Stubler and Jody Zamirowski from the College of DuPage. They deserve our gratitude for their work in cover design and graphics.

I am particularly grateful to the members of the National Council for Marketing and Public Relations. NCMPR is a strong advocate for America's community colleges and is totally committed to the advancement of the two-year college. Special thanks are in order to the many NCMPR members who contributed materials for possible use in the "sidebars and boxes" sections of this book.

To my good friend, Steve Lestarjette, I owe a debt of gratitude for his never ceasing encouragement and calm, reassuring leadership throughout this project. As president of the NCMPR, he has been the inspiration behind this team effort and a catalyst to this book, which initiates the organization's publication series. This series will add to the professional development services already provided by NCMPR for the hundreds of community college communicators who face the daily challenges of promoting their colleges to the public.

I am particularly grateful to the talented authors who worked closely with me to produce this book: Dr. George Boggs, Dr. Fred Snyder, Dr. Richard Fonte, Larry Bracken, Starnell Williams, Sandy Golden, and especially, Karen Jones, without whose persistence, good judgment, dedication to the task, and experience the book would never have been completed. I value their professionalism, patience, and willingness to serve as co-laborers in this joint venture. A debt of gratitude is also due Terri Baur for research assistance on exemplary programs.

I also wish to thank those colleagues at Phillips County Community College who gave their time to make the book eminently more readable: Steven Murray, Roma Richardson, Robin Bryant, David Durr, Kendra Moss, and particularly Janice Smith and Betsy Huff, for their extra efforts and encouragement. And I am grateful to the members of the PCCC Board of Trustees for their commitment and support. Dedicated community college trustees are essential to the success of the colleges they represent.

Finally, I am grateful to my family and children, Holly Rhea and Jennifer, for their willingness to share me with the work that too often directs my time and attention elsewhere. And I am eternally grateful to my wife, Tommye Lou, for her tolerance of my devotion to the other love of my life — the community college. She and I, and our daughters, continue to travel hopefully.

Steven W. Jones, Ed.D.
President
Phillips County Community College

CHAPTER 1

Institutional Image

by Fred A. Snyder, Ph.D.
Member, Board of Regents
Amarillo College

16

About the Author

Fred A. Snyder, Ph.D.

Fred A. Snyder is a member of the Board of Regents at Amarillo College (Texas) and operates his own management consulting business serving clients in business, education and other non-profit areas.

He earlier served two-year colleges and a state-wide community college system as an engineering instructor, dean of students, and director and vice president of planning and evaluation.

His education includes degrees in engineering, (B.S., Drexel University), student personnel services, and higher education and sociology (M.A. and Ph.D., University of Maryland).

Dr. Snyder has published numerous articles about the community college, including the role of the Board.

*T*he community college of the '90s has become a robust partner among educational institutions ranging from public schools to prestigious research universities. The community college is a 20th century phenomenon, unlike our public schools whose roots go back at least to the early 1800s, our public four-year colleges (many now called universities) whose roots emerged during the 19th century as "normal" schools for teacher preparation, and our research universities whose roots go back 900 years in Europe. It originally emerged from the secondary schools in some states and as a "junior college" truncated from the four-year college in others.

The community college is the adolescent among American educational institutions. Although a few had their origins in the early 1900s, 60 percent were founded just during the last 30 years. As is usually true of adolescents, the community college across the country is still unsure of its own identity. Other institutions and the general public are also unsure of what it is, partly because of its varied origins, partly because it continues to grow and change, and partly because of the breadth of its programs. The community college is vigorous, perhaps even lusty, but it lacks traditional guidelines as it responds to a rapidly changing world, even if its world is viewed primarily as regional, rather than national or global.

The community college is the most rapidly growing segment across the educational spectrum. It is a significant factor in American education and is becoming even more so. Both its student body and programs reflect diversity that 30 years ago would have been unthinkable in most parts of the country. Nationally, community colleges enroll about five million of the 13 million students at all colleges and universities. A majority of freshmen who enter higher education do so at community colleges. Because of its size, contribution to society, and potential growth, it is imperative that board members understand the nature of the community college and the issues and challenges which face it.

Nearly two decades ago, nine issues were listed as critical to the community college (Clyde B. Blocker, Robert H. Plummer, and Richard C. Richardson, Jr., *The Two-Year College: A Social Synthesis*, Prentice-Hall, 1965):

1. Maintaining comprehensive programs,
2. Serving well students with a wide variety of academic qualifications,
3. Adapting to changes in society versus becoming static,
4. Offering whatever programs the community wants while maintaining educational integrity,
5. Maintaining fiscal support,
6. Finding educational leaders to staff the colleges,
7. Creating effective patterns of administration and organization,
8. Avoiding division into vocational schools and college transfer schools, and
9. Acceptance by society that all persons have the right to education as far as they want to go.

These nine issues are still with us, but I suggest five more which also are of critical importance today:

10. Maintaining links to high schools and four-year colleges,
11. Maintaining links to employers and maintaining current knowledge of employment possibilities and careers,
12. Providing an effective pattern and practice of governance between state government and local community colleges,
13. Obtaining effective board leadership, and
14. Clarifying a vague, confused public image of the community college.

The last five issues emphasize maintaining links with schools, colleges and the institutions of employment; participation by state agencies in local college governance; board leadership; and clarifying the image of the community college. Together, these 14 issues reflect the basic concerns of boards, administrators and other educators who must work to achieve an effective, even outstanding, college.

The term "image" refers simply to a likeness, perception or representation of an object, process or event. Individuals experience reality only through their image of that reality, and the image usually reflects only a part of what might be perceived. The difficulty of matching image and reality is well documented. Image may be affected or distorted by: (1) the particular facets of the object which we observe; and (2) our mindset, context, or paradigm through which we interpret what we observe.

An image of the community college may focus on one or more facets, such as admission and placement policies, educational programs, student characteristics, faculty, campus and facilities, graduates, history and purpose, publications, and others. The image may be viewed by different groups, such as current students, prospective students, college staff, school staff, parents, former students, taxpayers, homeowners, legislators, local office holders, employers, business groups, agency groups, four-year college and university staff, prospective donors, and, of course, community college board members. These viewers represent different interests (mindsets, contexts, paradigms) and they see different facets. You can be sure their images of the community college differ greatly.

The purpose of this book is to demonstrate to board members and educators at the community college the importance of the community college image, to review the conditions affecting its image, and to identify the effort needed to align the college image in the community with the reality of the college as an effective and valuable institution.

Historical Development

The term "community college" is relatively new. Although it appears in the literature several times as early as the 1930s, it wasn't until the 1960s, a decade during which nearly half of all the public two-year colleges were formed, that "community college" regularly appeared in the names of these institutions. Prior to then the most common term, applied to public and private two-year colleges alike, was "junior college." Today, the term community college is also sometimes used as an umbrella to include both public and private colleges, public technical colleges and occasionally even proprietary schools. However, seven of every eight two-year colleges are public, and since there are relatively few technical schools, the term usually applies to public two-year colleges which offer a comprehensive array of programs in career and technical, college transfer and community service areas.

The purpose of this book precludes space for a detailed history of the development of the modern community college. However, many board members may find such a history valuable in understanding better the colleges they now govern. Therefore, I recommend three sources, each of which is readable and should be available in the local college library:

James W. Thornton, Jr, *The Community Junior College*, 2nd edition, John Wiley & Sons, 1966, pp. 45-57.
George B. Vaughan, *The Community College in America: A Short History*, 3rd printing, revised, AACJC, 1985, pp. 1-25.
Arthur M. Cohen and Florence B. Brawer, *The American Community College*, 2nd edition, Jossey-Bass, 1989, pp. 1-29.

Probably the most practical for board members, both to obtain and read, is George Vaughan's slim 25-page booklet. It combines a good historical overview with current (1985) issues which confront the community college.

The roots of today's community colleges are diverse, due to differences in state enabling legislation and earlier occurrences of seminal leadership by leaders at major universities. The basic roots include:

• Truncated versions of small, struggling four-year colleges in which the last two years of the baccalaureate had been discontinued, leaving the freshman and sophomore years standing,
• New junior colleges formed by religious groups to serve

regional clusters of members,
• Extensions of the usual public high school level, created
either by offering college-level honors courses in the school or
by creating separate junior colleges under the control of school
districts,
• Two-year branch campuses or centers created by existing
colleges or universities to offer freshman and sophomore level
courses or special technical programs,
• State legislation which empowered cities or regions to create
junior college (community college) taxing districts and begin
new colleges, and
• State legislation which created new regional community
college districts and state funding to support them.

It may be of interest to note the dates of legislation which
empowered public two-year colleges in several states. The first was
California (1907); followed by Michigan and Kansas (1917); Arizona,
Minnesota and Missouri (1920s); New York (1949); Florida (1950s);
New Jersey, Pennsylvania and Virginia (1960s). The northeast
region of the country was the last to obtain state legislation and
support. This region had earlier developed a system of private and
public higher education, and the newer community college was
resisted as a competitor for limited state funds and student enrollment. Cohen and Brawer (1989) noted four stages of community
college development to include the extensions of secondary schools
(1910-30), formation of separate districts (1930-50), state-level
coordination (1950-70) and increased state control and funding,
including institutional consolidation (1970-present).

The vast majority (90 percent) of the 1200 plus community
colleges were created either by public school districts or as separate
community college districts during the 1930s through the 1970s.
The number of private two-year colleges reached a maximum of
just over 300 in the late 1940s, and has since declined to about 160.
Enrollment figures show an even greater preponderance of public
community colleges. In 1989, public two-year college enrollments
exceeded 4.8 million. Private two-year college enrollments totalled
about 260,000, or 5 percent of all two-year enrollments.

Educational Values

Several key values have emerged over the decades and continue to guide the development of the community college:

- Comprehensive educational program
- Access to educational opportunity
- Improving quality of life
- Economic development
- Local support and control

Comprehensive educational program. The educational program of the two-year college has evolved from a strictly "collegiate level" program for transfer to four-year colleges to a comprehensive curriculum. This curriculum now includes programs and courses in general education, liberal arts, cultural and social education, fine arts, scientific studies, technical education, and vocational training.

Access to education. A major impetus to the value of open access to higher education was provided by the 1947 report of the Truman Commission, which recommended establishing a network of low-cost community colleges across the country. Open access to all who wish to continue their education remains a cardinal value of the community college movement. As a result, the community college has for decades maintained special programs in counseling and guidance to help students explore their educational and career goals and acquire the means to reach these goals. Low cost of tuition and fees is a primary supporting value and, as a result, these costs remain well under $500 per semester at many two-year colleges. Unfortunately, some colleges, typically in the northeast, are forced to charge student fees sometimes in excess of $1,000 per semester. Other efforts to maximize access have included building college campuses in population centers rather than fringe locations; providing financial grants and loans from local, as well as state and federal, sources; locating child care centers on college campuses; and providing an extensive program of compensatory learning skills for adults in areas of reading, mathematics and writing.

Special programs of support are often directed to adult women and minority groups. Across the country women comprise about 60 percent of community college enrollment. Minority enrollment is proportionally higher at community colleges than at four-year colleges and universities. Much of this success in enrolling women and minorities is due to policies and programs developed in deliber-ate support of open access. It is interesting to note that Miami-Dade Community College was the first public school or college in Florida to enroll both black and white students; it opened as an integrated institution in 1960.

Improving quality of life. The entire array of educational programs and services at the community college addresses the value that education contributes to the quality of life for individuals and community. In addition to transfer and occupational-technical programs, special emphasis is placed on adult literacy, continuing adult learning, and learning experiences, regardless of their formal credit value or qualification for state funding. The community college appears well-placed to provide opportunities for lifelong learning, for purposes of general quality of life and continued career growth.

Economic development, or support for business and industry. The traditional credit programs of technical education and vocational skills training were supplemented in the 1980s with special courses in training managers, supervisors, small business owners and prospective entrepreneurs. More recently, courses and programs have been added in areas of specific job skills, workplace safety, environmental hazards and environmental control. Such efforts toward economic development may be comprised of credit and non-credit courses, or customized training programs.

Local support and control. Emphasis on local support (funding) and control (governance) has been a long-standing cardinal value of the community college.   Tuition and fees charged to students, al-though low compared to those charged at public four-year colleges, vary considerably from state to state. During 1991-92, community college students in California paid under $200 per year; students in states like Arizona, Arkansas, Kansas and Texas paid $300 to $900; in New York and Pennsylvania, they paid $1,200 to $2,000; and several colleges in Massachusetts charged over $2,000 *(1993 Higher Education Directory*, by Higher Education Publications, Inc.). In many states, the ideal funding mix is for local tax rates and student tuition to comprise half or less of total community college revenues, with state appropriations providing the remainder. Typically, colleges with low student fees receive more state funds than those which charge higher fees. Additional federal funding for student grants and loans, plus earmarked funding for exemplary or developmental projects, serve to supplement state and local support.

In most states, control of the programs and operation of the community college is granted to a local governing board, which is also granted authority to raise taxes and set tuition rates. Unfortunately for local control and funding, state governments are taking a far heavier role in coordinating and regulating college operations, while at the same time reducing their support for local college budgets. To some extent, the loss of state funds is being supplemented by more intensive local efforts to secure contributions from private sources. Private foundations have been established at hundreds of community colleges to assist in these fundraising efforts.

The Educational Program

The diversity of educational programs and services at the comprehensive community college is difficult to grasp because it is untraditional (compared to that of the high school and the four-year college and university). The following brief portrayal of the programs offered by a typical community college sets the stage for better understanding the challenges facing community colleges as they seek to present an accurate image to the public.

A community college is chartered or created for specific purposes. The educational programs offered by a college should reflect its purposes. The relationship between purpose and programs may be illustrated best by showing the list of purposes which are mandated or recommended for community colleges in a given state (Texas), followed by a list of the educational programs at one college in that state:

> A public junior college is an institution of higher learning, controlled by a local board of trustees or regents, and operated under statutory provisions. A public junior college may confer associate degrees, but does not grant the baccalaureate degree.

> The purpose of each public community college shall be to provide:
> (1) technical programs up to two years in length leading to associate degrees or certificates;
> (2) vocational programs leading directly to employment in semi-skilled and skilled occupations;
> (3) freshman and sophomore courses in arts and sciences;
> (4) continuing adult education programs for occupational or cultural upgrading;
> (5) compensatory education programs designed to fulfill the commitment of an admissions policy allowing the enrollment of disadvantaged students;
> (6) a continuing program of counseling and guidance designed to assist students in achieving their individual educational goals;
> (7) workforce development programs designed to meet local and statewide needs; and
> (8) literacy and other basic skills programs to prepare adults to live more functionally.

> (Purposes (1) through (6) are mandated by the Texas Higher Education Coordinating Board, and purposes (7) and (8) are recommended by the Texas Public Community Junior College Association)

Trustees and regents should become familiar with the educational programs offered by their respective colleges by reading the catalog and related documents.

Figure 1. Educational Programs at Amarillo College

Occupational-Technical Programs

Allied Health

Dental hygiene
Medical information
Medical lab technician
Paramedic technician

Pharmacy technician
Physical therapist assistant
Physical/occupational therapist
Radiation therapy
Radiography

Respiratory care
Surgical technician
Veterinary assistant

Engineering & Industrial Technology

Air conditioning/ refrigeration
Auto/diesel repair
Drafting/CAD
Electrical/electronic instrmentation
Fire protection
Hazardous materials
Industrial maintenance
Architecture
Electronics engineering technology
Electronics technology
Engineering technology

Business

Accounting
Business management
Computer information systems
Computer operator/data processing

Nursing

Assoc. degree nursing (RN)
Vocational nursing (LVN)

Others

Office occupations
Secretarial (several)
Word processing
Court reporting
Real estate
Retail merchandising
Travel and tourism

Child care assistant
Criminal justice
Substance abuse counselor
Photography
Radio-television production
Commercial art

Transfer Programs

Education
Home Economics
Liberal arts
Physical education
Social sciences
Computer information systems
Biological sciences

Sciences and engineering
Pre-professional
Pre-nursing (BSN)
Art
Journalism
Business administration
Management

Other Enrollments

Basic learning skills
No declared program

The list of credit programs at one Texas college (Amarillo College), shown in Figure 1, illustrates the variety and number of occupational-technical and transfer programs leading to an associate degree or certificate. These programs relate directly to purposes (1), (2) and (3).

The occupational-technical programs typically lead to a two-year associate degree, but in some instances students may complete an abbreviated program and be awarded a certificate of completion. The terms "technical" and "vocational" are often used to distinguish between programs with a basis in mathematics and the sciences (technical) and those based on common industrial practice (vocational) more than on math and science. "Vocational" programs typically refer to preparation for employment in semi-skilled and skilled occupations. They usually lead to a certificate of completion rather than a two-year associate degree. Taken together, the occupational-technical programs relate to purposes (1) and (2).

The transfer programs (3) are always designed to transfer to four-year colleges and universities, although some students who may not intend to pursue a bachelor's degree enroll in "transfer" courses. Also, transfer courses, such as those in English, mathematics, social sciences, speech and communication, life sciences, and natural sciences, serve as the general education component of associate degree programs in occupational-technical areas.

To make the distinction between occupational-technical and transfer programs even less clear, students who complete occupational-technical programs may transfer to four-year institutions to receive bachelors degrees in technical areas. Examples of such four-year technical programs include physical therapy, nursing, engineering technology, bachelor of applied sciences, computer information systems, and vocational education. No longer is enrollment in an occupational-technical program necessarily a "terminal" educational decision, as was commonly thought several decades ago.

Purpose (4), continuing adult education, may be fulfilled by enrollments in courses or programs offered to meet the first three purposes plus special courses which are not part of an existing program.

Compensatory education programs (5) focus on providing basic learning skills in reading, writing and mathematics, and occasionally in occupational-specific fields of study.

Counseling and guidance (6) are available to all students. Such services typically include guidance in examining employment possibilities and careers, relating these to existing educational programs, and making personal selections of career and educational programs. Services often include explaining the placement testing program used to determine the student's readiness to enter a given academic program and the readiness criteria for beginning a program, identifying special individual problems where psychological counseling or other forms of assistance may be needed, and obtaining professional assistance not offered by the college.

Other services provided at most community colleges include identifying the need for special support such as financial assistance, child care, and part-time employment. An extensive program of student support services is also offered at the typical college in order to enhance students' likelihood of educational success. Support services include a comprehensive program of federal, state and local financial aids, student activities, intramural athletics (especially for the younger students), sometimes intercollegiate athletics, student government, job placement and others. Many colleges offer special support and activity programs for older students, including counseling and assistance programs for single mothers, displaced homemakers, and those seeking or forced into a change of careers.

Workforce development programs (7) are intended to meet the needs of specific employers or employer groups. Such programs may be designed uniquely or they may be comprised of existing courses in areas such as work skills, supervisory development, safety, and management development. Workforce development programs are typically carried out under contract between the college and a specific business, business group or business development agency. Such programs may start with immediate short-term objectives and evolve into ongoing programs to include enrollments in standard curricula, with the employer paying all or much of the enrollment costs for individual employees.

In regions with high rates of functional illiteracy and inadequate basic learning skills among adults, special programs (8) are offered to adults by the community colleges directly, or in cooperation with other educational and social agencies, as a means to enhance individual lives, community development or economic development. Programs in adult basic education, English as a second language, and preparation for the GED high school equivalency are typically offered. The community college may also offer, often with other agencies, life skill programs such as job seeking, managing personal finances, and child care, just to name a few.

Outreach and community service programs. In addition to formally structured educational programs and courses, community colleges offer a variety of community service programs to the regions they serve. The nature of these service programs will vary from college to college, depending on characteristics and needs of the service region and the college's unique strengths. A list of one college's programs (Amarillo College) will serve to illustrate the nature and breadth of what are commonly called "outreach and community service programs." Figure 2 shows a broad variety of programs, some highly structured and others occasional. Programs cover operation of public radio and TV stations, performing arts, nationally known speakers on topics of culture and current events, programs for area school students and for staff development, outreach to minority neighborhoods, and presentations of interest to business and industry.

Claims for Effectiveness

I have noted briefly the history, values and educational programs of the community college. Since the college is a relative newcomer to public education, it is important to understand its claims for effectiveness and value to individuals and society. There is accumulated evidence to document the contributions of the community college, but there are also critics. A summary of key criticisms follows this section. Governing boards and educators at the community college must be aware of both its effectiveness and critics in order to direct and operate it wisely.

Some of the basic claims for effectiveness are that community colleges:

1. *Extend opportunity for post-high school and college-level education to more people.* The community college claims to increase the rate of college attendance and provide its benefits to individuals who, for whatever reason, would not attend college without the presence of a local community college. These include adults who did not attend college upon graduation from high school; those who are disadvantaged financially, culturally or socio-economically; those whose school achievement record may indicate the need for compensatory work prior to admission into a college-level program; and those who qualify to attend a four-year institution, but, because the community college is located near their home, find it more practical to attend there.

2. *Maintain excellence across a comprehensive curriculum.* The community college claims to educate and train its students successfully in diverse program areas of occupational-technical education, transfer to senior institutions, compensatory educational and coping skills, adult continuing education, workforce training and community services. It claims that its students remain enrolled at the community college until their reasons for attending are met (the open door is not a revolving door). It claims that its graduates obtain and hold jobs in areas related to their curriculum and that its transfer students enroll in senior colleges, where they succeed as well as native enrollees. It claims that disadvantaged students are provided appropriate guidance, learning experiences and assistance to enable them to benefit from community college education, and that they often complete program objectives of occupational-technical education or transfer to senior colleges.

3. *Keep student costs low.* Community colleges claim to provide their educational programs at considerably less cost than do

four-year colleges and universities. The student pays much lower tuition and fees and often saves residential expenses by living at home.

4. *Provide quick response to local needs.* The community college claims to respond quickly to local or regional educational needs by developing academic courses, curricula or short courses, and delivering them to the point of need.

Figure 2. Outreach and Community Service Programs at Amarillo College

Radio/TV stations
> Public radio station
> Public (PBS) TV station

Arts and Humanities
> Amarillo Opera
> Art workshops
> Summer Arts Festival
> College Theater
> Amarillo Art Center
> Amarillo Children's Theater
> Student art show
> Creative Mind lecture series
> Private music lessons

Programs for area schools
> Science and technology programs for elementary students
> Scholars Program for gifted high school students
> Tex PREP summer program for disadvantaged middle and senior students to explore science and engineering careers
> Tech-prep program with area schools to develop interest in technical programs
> Literary and speech competition for students at area schools
> Student publications workshops
> Regional science fair
> Teachers institute for high school math teachers

Adult & Community Outreach
> Adult learning center in North Branch YMCA (Amarillo); Tulia, TX; and Hereford, TX
> STAR awareness programs for Hispanic community
> Book reviews, via radio and meeting forums
> Early morning forums on business and industry topics
> Workshops on counseling and human relationship topics for schools and general public
> Distinguished Lecture Series

The Criticisms

Educators are occupied with maintaining their institutional mission and programs, and with daily operations over sustained periods. They may become oblivious to real weaknesses which are visible to outside eyes. It is important that educators and board members, who are concerned about their college's image and effectiveness, be aware of thoughtful criticism, as it can be a useful tool for focusing on institutional weakness and the need for improvement. Criticism can come from those who simply don't understand the community college, from those who fear change or institutional competition, or from responsible community college educators and informed scholars who have extensive experience with the community college. The criticisms of several well-known responsible critics are summarized in the paragraphs which follow:

> L. Steven Zwerling, *Second Best: The Crisis of the Community College*, McGraw Hill, 1976. Zwerling worked as an educator at an inner city community college in New York. He maintained that the community college was not succeeding in its social goal of providing inner city families the opportunity for a college education, based on high dropout rates and low frequency of transfer to four-year colleges. Instead, he claimed that the aspirations of such students were merely being trimmed to a "realistic" level.

> Richard C. Richardson, Jr., Elizabeth C. Fisk and Morris A. Okun, *Literacy in the Open-Access College*, Jossey-Bass, 1983. Richardson had served as a community college dean and president in two states, and more recently served as professor and chair of the Department of Higher and Adult Education at Arizona State University. His two colleagues also served on the education faculty at the same university. Their criticism was that the community college, in its efforts to educate growing numbers of students with weak communication skills, has relaxed its standards of critical reading and writing. They also suggested corrective measures.

Dennis McGrath and Martin B. Spear, *The Academic Crisis of the Community College*, State University of New York Press, 1991. McGrath and Spear are faculty members at the Community College of Philadelphia, serving in departments of social science and history and philosophy. They maintain that community colleges are often unsuccessful with untraditional inner city students, not because of intent, but from a misunderstanding of the problems such students face. They call for more attention to "constructing bridges" to connect students' non-traditional, disadvantaged backgrounds with the educated, learning community which the college represents.

Steven Brint and Jerome Karabel, *The Diverted Dream*, Oxford, 1989. Brint and Karabel were professors of sociology at Yale and the University of California-Berkeley, respectively. Whereas the three previous critics have extensive experience inside the community college, Brint and Karabel viewed it from the perspective of social theory and the prestigious university. They stated that as the community college shifted its emphasis from liberal arts to "terminal vocational programs" during the previous 20 years, it has actually served to divert the majority of its students from a four-year education.

The criticisms by the above four groups of authors can be summarized:

- Educational aspirations of many students are not being realized; instead those aspirations are being trimmed to a "realistic" level, more in line with their current disadvantaged existence. Inner city students are not benefitting from attending the community college.

- The community college has reduced the level of its educational program to accommodate students with weak communication skills, and as a result, has reduced its effectiveness for all students.

- The college has not learned to help disadvantaged students "bridge" their non-traditional family and community culture with the culture and expectations of the college — the instructor, assumptions about the value of classroom learning, the discipline of time and task, and the ultimate meaning and value of learning and knowledge.

- The community college has diverted a majority of its students from a four-year college education by placing emphasis on "terminal vocational programs."

Several of these criticisms imply that community colleges are more responsive to the criterion of enrollment, rather than criteria for learning effectiveness, because enrollment drives state appropriations for public colleges in most states. Fortunately, agencies of higher education in numerous states are working with college administrators on a transition to "effectiveness" outcomes, rather than enrollments alone, as a basis for funding. This transition will not be easy. Practical problems include which criteria of effectiveness to use, how to measure them, and how they are to be weighed in funding decisions. The cost of expanding existing efforts to evaluate outcomes at local colleges will be considerable. However, as a related benefit of such efforts, colleges are more likely to consider redesigning or discontinuing programs which do not produce effective results.

Community colleges enroll large numbers of disadvantaged students. They attempt to prepare these students for success by offering a variety of special programs - compensatory programs in language, writing and mathematics; English as a second language; special guidance and counseling classes; and various life skills programs. They attempt to place students at the most appropriate level in compensatory programs through validated pre-placement tests. But, several of the critics claim that these attempts are not effective. McGrath and Spear call for carefully-conceived programs which will allow students to "bridge" their existing non-traditional family and community culture with the culture and expectations of the learning community. Such an approach may demand a stronger effort, with counselors and classroom teachers working together, to build effective programs for students who are not now well served. Not doing so may lead to a decision to retrench efforts to educate disadvantaged people.

Critics of the community college often imply that it tries to "be all things to all people." The charge may be linked to the breadth of curricula and levels of courses. The college offers programs across a broad spectrum of purposes and it also offers courses at several levels of purpose and intensity, particularly in subject areas of English, mathematics and the sciences, but also in occupational courses. In part, this criticism results from comparing the community college program with that of the four-year college, where both the range of programs and the levels of courses (and student preparedness) are more constrained. It may also result from comparing the community college with the technical institute or other types of special-purpose institutions.

Regardless of the comparative context, the criticism hits at the heart of effectiveness and is valid to the extent that students are enrolled in courses they fail to finish, withdraw from the college without fulfilling a valid educational purpose for being there, or, once completing a program, they are unable to progress into a meaningful career or continue their educational development. It should be noted that such outcomes occur at four-year colleges as well, and are not limited to two-year colleges.

Breadth of curricula, various levels of course rigor and various levels of student "readiness," are not necessarily weaknesses of the community college. We know enough about organizational effectiveness to be able to provide for many objectives, provided that each objective is well understood, is the responsibility of qualified staff, and has adequate resources available to carry it out. A recent case study of Miami-Dade Community College portrays how one of the nation's largest community college operates to be also, in the opinion of many educators, the nation's best (John E. Roueche and George A Baker III, *Access & Excellence: The Open Door College*, Community College Press, 1987). Size does not work against excellence; it may actually enhance it. The key is to create an organization whose climate, leadership, approach to teaching, and support systems are constantly directed to the success of its students and to articulate these qualities as part of the public image.

Community college costs are less than those at four-year colleges and universities, both to state legislatures who appropriate funds for them and to students who pay tuition. To cut costs even further, many community colleges use part-time faculty, who cost much less per course, to teach large numbers of classes. In some states, appropriations have been reduced to the point where the alternative to using part-time faculty is simply not to offer the course. It is not clear that using some part-time faculty will reduce the quality of student learning, but logic suggests that at some level of increased use the effectiveness of the educational program will be reduced. *Community colleges should direct serious attention to investigating the relationship between the use of part-time faculty and both student learning outcomes and long-term college effectiveness.*

The criticisms just presented are by writers of differing backgrounds and are sometimes based on community college environments which may not be typical. It is not my purpose to critique the critics, but rather to point out potential weaknesses, along with strengths, of our colleges.

Shaping the Community College Image

Community college educators must accept the need to shape the accuracy and vitality of the image the college projects to prospective students, employers, agencies and taxpayers. Such effort is necessary during today's emphasis on marketing and selling goods and services by the commercial and institutional world. The college must go beyond simply informing others about what it does and the way it operates; it must also maintain dialogue with regional entities and individuals about their needs. The process of shaping and projecting the college's image allows exchange of information between users and the college, and assists the college in continually developing effective programs and maintaining support for them.

Several recommendations follow as a guide to shaping the community college image:

The image must focus on each of the college's primary educational programs. The array of programs at the community college is so broad that efforts to inform people by generalizing about them will have but limited success. It has been said that the support for one well-established community college is "a mile wide and an inch deep," meaning that people have a warm feeling about it, but cannot sustain that feeling by specific examples of programs it offers or value it produces.

The college should focus the image on those key qualities or resources which sustain its success. Most important among these is the faculty and professional staff, perhaps followed by campuses and physical facilities, student support services, community services and other supporting aspects. The college should also identify and highlight its "centers of excellence," but without removing the focus from those qualities or resources which will continue to sustain the success of the institution.

The image must focus on the college's successes and achievements. Examples include evidences of student success (grade point average, retention, graduation rate, subsequent employment and college transfer data), the proportion or market share of all regional students who are enrolled at the local community college, degrees awarded, fund development, improvements in programs and facilities, honors and recognitions.

It is important that successes and achievements of students be well documented through a system of evaluation, as such information also serves the crucial process of making continuous improvement. The fact is, when we look at student outcomes we find both successes and occasional failures. *Without specific outcomes data to guide them, organizations tend to continue current practices, beliefs and programs long beyond their period of usefulness.* Organizations tend to stay within a familiar comfort zone rather than undergo change, even if current results are less than ideal.

Educational programs and support systems of doubtful value should be revised or discarded. Otherwise, the image will reflect a college which is not well-run, at least in some aspects.

Image will not be projected well by relying primarily on occasional stories written by the staff or by media representatives. The shaping of an accurate, useful image must be perceived as a program which requires careful planning and action, for several reasons: (a) We want precise, significant information about our programs and operation to go to prospective students, schools, employers, community groups and taxpayers. (b) We want employers and four-year colleges to trust the quality of our students on the basis of our certification, and that trust is enhanced when, over the years, the claims we project are validated by experience. (c) We want the supporting public (taxpayers, legislators, agencies and donors) to see the college as valuable and as a good steward of its resources. (d) Finally, we want to create among taxpayers an awareness that they own a valuable local college.

Image must focus on outcomes, as well as on use of resources. It must emphasize value added, return on investment, efficiency and effectiveness in accomplishing the college's mission and program objectives. This focus calls for a valid, precise ap-proach to measurement and evaluation. All colleges produce an annual operating statement: a numerical account of their dollar resources received, an allocation of these dollars to specific activities, and a summary of deficit or excess. They also produce an annual balance sheet: a list of the dollar value of assets, liabilities and special fund accounts. Unfortunately, few colleges produce an effective annual report to show how well they have fulfilled their mission during the year. Although some community colleges have been developing models of institutional effectiveness over recent years, it is a sad fact that many will act only in response to pressure by state agencies or other external sources rather than their own motives for institutional improvement.

The community college board is responsible for approving policy and programs of the college, hiring the president, and overseeing the effectiveness of the college operation. In practice, the board assigns responsibility and authority to operate the college to the president. The president and the college staff actually develop college policies, the annual budget and perhaps multi-year capital budgets, educational programs and support systems for board approval. Still, *boards have a responsibility they cannot fully delegate, namely, to see to the long-range development and effectiveness of the college.*

This responsibility includes creation of an accurate, relevant image of college programs, services and vitality for users and supporters in its service region. This image will serve to: (1) maintain relationships with government agencies charged with support and control of the college, (2) support the marketing, public relations and funds development efforts of the college to attract students and community support, and (3) guide and support the dialogue between college and community about the needs of the community, and the need for revised or new programs and services.

Getting To Know Your Neighborhoods

Niagara County Community College's image in the community was for the most part very positive. However, we were bothered by the fact that our efforts were always enticing the public to come to us and felt we needed to get to know them better by going to them.

In 1990 we embarked on a two-year "In Your Neighborhood" program. The focus of the program was to visit each of more than a dozen towns and villages in Niagara County and do something special with them. A steering committee dealt with the program objectives, theme and graphics and support materials, and set up meetings with employees representing each community.

The program's grand opening was held at the county fair; we provided entertainment and decorated our booth to look like a front porch, where our president served free lemonade. From there our representative employees met with community leaders to determine the joint ventures the college could share with the community.

Outreach activities included providing craft demonstrations, the haunting of a mansion by our theatre department to raise funds for the mansion's renovation, participating in elementary and high school fairs, festivals and parades, and creation of a video with a group of elementary school students. We also met with business people informally to discuss how we could assist them and in some cases helped raise scholarship funds for students from their community.

Each community contact program lasted at least a month and included recognition of outstanding alumni, local school teachers who our students said had a major impact on their lives, and families whose members have had varied relationships with the college. Along with the community visits, we produced a cable television program called N-Triple-Scene, which runs weekly on our local cable stations. The entire program is done in-house by our audio visual department.

In October, 1992, we had a grand finale of the program by sponsoring a Family Fun and Fitness Fair on our campus. We invited back each community we visited and recognized them. Each community brought a gift which will be on permanent display in our college library. Community groups participated by setting up booths, and entertainment was provided by various groups from the communities. Over 2,000 people attended.

We feel the results of this program were very positive. Faculty, staff, students and administrators went to communities they normally wouldn't visit, meeting new people and having new experiences. People now know that NCCC is more than just a college and comment on how talented our student performers are and how energetic our staff is. We have also heard, "I didn't know NCCC had....." Now they know. And we know each other's needs.

by Janet Schultz
Public Relations Technical Assistant
Niagara County Community College
Sanbom, New York

Trustees' Tips for Interaction

Trustees are often the people with the credibility and reputation to be the best cheerleaders and storytellers for community colleges. Through their community activities—especially those as representatives of their college—trustees can enhance their institution's image. Trustees can maximize their role as positive image builders for the community college movement by taking advantage of local opportunities. Here are several suggestions to help trustees do just that:

- Be generous with your business cards. As an ambassador of community relations on the college's behalf, open the door for interaction.
- Join the college's speakers bureau and make presentations to local service clubs and organizations. Gather stories about the college which underscore the institution's successes, illustrating abstract statistics with real life stories about teachers and students.
- Become an expert in some aspect of the college's operations and practice speaking in headlines and soundbites. For example, what impacts would the community face if the college closed its doors tomorrow?
- Seek active memberships on chamber of commerce committees, economic development councils, and the mayor's and governor's advisories.
- Attend events sponsored by the college—plays, sports events, receptions, open houses. Your appearance at events is a morale booster and a major source of pride for both employees and students.
- Write letters to employees and students lauding their accomplishments and to people in the news who do

something of note for education. Handwritten notes make lasting impressions on recipients.
- Keep your college relations office informed about your civic contributions so they can be shared with internal and external publics through employee and student publications and college-generated publicity.

by Dr. Joyce Boatright
Vice Chancellor, Institutional Advancement
North Harris Montgomery Community College District
Houston, Texas

CHAPTER 2

Research and the Community College Image

by Richard Fonte, Ph.D.
President
South Suburban College

About the Author

Dr. Richard Fonte

As president of South Suburban College, South Holland, Illinois, Fonte initiated a comprehensive institutional renewal program including an aggressive external relations effort. These community college image enhancement activities involved implementation of a name-change for the college, sophisticated direct mail marketing, a state legislative and community relations program, and the establishment of a fund-raising foundation.

Dr. Fonte is a past president of the National Council for Marketing and Public Relations and frequently makes presentations on community college marketing.

*I*t can be said that the image of a community college is the summary judgment of the quality perceived in the programs and services of that institution. In that case, a community college must be able to answer questions on how well, or with what quality, it is carrying out its purposes or missions. Such questions of quality arise from the various publics who interact with the community college. A positive image is achieved if satisfactory answers are provided to these multiple publics.

Research analysis assists colleges to determine whether critical publics perceive institutional responses to be adequate over a broad time period. Community college professionals interested in image enhancement for their institutions must become familiar not only with how to determine the reactions of these publics, but also with what institutional research is essential to provide colleges with satisfactory answers to key publics. In particular, those responsible for image enhancement must become partners with institutional research personnel in developing a strategy for communicating key answers to questions of institutional quality.

The multiple missions of a community college complicate both the ability to communicate a positive institutional image and to carry out the research needed to demonstrate quality delivery of programs and services. Each community college serves differently the educational needs of its local area. This diversity is one of the strengths of locally responsive community colleges. It is, however, also the source of confusion over community college effectiveness and image in the eyes of the national media, public policy makers, and the general public.

The importance of research to assist community colleges to systematically project a sustained positive "image" in their local community is evident in an environment that "cannot be transformed by a single positive or negative image-producing incident" (Alfred, 1987). In such an environment, public relations activities unguided by a long-range plan based upon institutional research will inevitably fail.

Kotler (1975) suggested that a college's distinct publics involve external groups such as the business community, governmental entities including the legislature and funding agencies along with internal groups including faculty, students, administration and staff. He also suggested that these various publics have different levels of interest and involvement with the college which will impact their institutional impression and will influence the overall public image of the college. Because of the complexity of the interaction between multiple publics, Alfred (1987) has suggested that a sustained "image" (which he defines as "stature") is resistent to change.

Comparison of Market and Image Research

The research required to advance a sustained effort to improve a college's "image" differs from research required solely for student recruitment marketing. While student recruitment marketing research places a priority focus on the concerns of a few publics, image research requires an analysis of many more publics. Student recruitment marketing research places an emphasis on analysis of factors related to enrollment. These include students as consumers, current and potential, and publics such as parents and high school counselors who closely influence student decisions to enroll at a college. The bottom line in student recruitment market research is the market share of enrollment achieved for a targeted sub-part of the population. In contrast image research broadens the definition of the "customer" of the college beyond the direct consumer of educational courses and programs. Any individuals or publics who have an actual or potential interest or impact upon the college are "image customers" of the college. Thus, the publics interested in image are broadened to include funding authorities, the business community, the general community and others.

The analyses and related activities of student recruitment research and image research are, of course, not unconnected. Obviously, the overall image of an institution will impact individual student enrollment decisions. A "marketing orientation," a critical factor in successful student recruitment efforts, may also positively affect successful foundation donor drives from the business community or the passage of a referendum. Moreover, "image" advertising based upon projecting a positive impression of the institution often is interconnected with any student recruitment marketing campaign. In fact, a strong case can be made for continuous "image" oriented advertising even when enrollments are high, to communicate to the college's community the on-going efforts of the college to fulfill its multiple missions.

Alfred (1987) has warned that the public perception of post-secondary education can "change rapidly and that institutions are never secure in the eyes of the public." Consequently, on-going public relations, image-enhancing activities have the dual purpose of communicating an image and building a climate favorable to improved student recruitment. The bottom line for an institution concerning its "image customers" is whether they have a favorable impression of the institution. "Image" research aims to determine whether this has been achieved, and whether activities or actions of the college have moved the particular public toward a more favorable impression of the college.

Research Challenges to Community College Image

In the so-called golden age of community college growth (in the early '60s to mid-'70s), positive trends in enrollments and a positive image of community colleges seemed to go together. Enrollment growth research and market share analysis demonstrating increased access by "non-traditional" minority students and "returning women" were used to project a positive image for community colleges. Anecdotal "research," examples or case studies highlighting these trends, were forms of image research and image communication.

During the next period of community college evolution running into the mid-'80s, both enrollment fluctuations and disputes over the community college successfully fulfilling its purposes became more common (Tillery and Deegan, 1985). The current period of community college development, tightened financial resources and a rise of community college critics (Clark, 1980; Zwerling, 1976) has led to a demand for greater accountability by community colleges and for research measures other than those demonstrating access. In fact, the critics suggest that the image of "access" was a myth and that minorities, in particular, may be thwarted in obtaining a baccalaureate degree if they begin their college education at a community college. Anecdotal "research" examples have become frequently used by the media to negatively impact community college image.

The American Association of Community Colleges (AACC) in 1992 adopted a statement which calls for the use of multiple research measures to determine institutional effectiveness. Despite this AACC position, members of the media and the public policy and research community regularly take actions, either consciously or unconsciously, that advance a single measure of success.

The current trend among the "image" critics of community colleges is to first constrict community college mission by focusing on the transfer of community college students to four-year universities and colleges. All other missions, such as career education or contract training for business and industry or community education, are relegated to a secondary position.

Media Attention Toward the Transfer Image

Effectiveness of the transfer mission threatens to become the pervasive research measure to evaluate institutional effectiveness for community colleges and the creation of a successful or failing "image" for community colleges.

Why is this?

One answer lies with the critical role played in image creation by journalists. Journalists prefer the convenience of communicating clearly and simply with "shorthand" measures of success. Educational media writers tend to conceptualize colleges as degree-producing organizations, perhaps because of their own higher educational experiences. Degrees represent a "successful" product and a clear, definable outcome for a college.

The degree most closely associated with "college" is, of course, the baccalaureate degree. Since community colleges don't grant this degree, educational writers have gravitated to the use of a supplemental "proxy" yardstick, the transfer rate. This rate establishes a link between the Bachelor's degree and community colleges. With the media's perception of "college" and the Bachelor's degree highly interconnected, "success" at the community college level has become dominated by emphasis on the transfer mission or programs leading to the eventual achievement of a Bachelor's degree.

Image research activities and image enhancement by community college professionals must, therefore, be cognizant of the current mass media environment influencing community college image development. While the media is not the only public critical to community college image enhancement, they clearly impact the reaction of other key publics or image "customers" of the college, particularly legislative and other public officials.

Because of this media orientation, image enhancement will require positive answers to be provided to questions of transfer effectiveness. These answers must begin to be provided through communication of "hard" information regarding transfer outcomes to critical publics. We must be able to answer the question of how many of our students transfer and how well they do once they transfer. Critical publics, such as governmental agencies, legislators, potential foundation donors, will alter their impression of our institution based upon "satisfactory" responses to these questions.

Research Essential to Image Communications

Public relations efforts have long attempted, with varying degrees of success, to portray in the media positive images which chronicle outcomes of the colleges engaged in transfer preparation, career education, remedial or adult basic education, worker retraining economic development and other aspects of a comprehensive community college image. Frequently these "chronicles" have relied upon "anecdotal research" or examples of positive outcomes in these areas. In the future such case study or anecdotal research will be inadequate for the public relations office to carry out its image communication responsibilities.

Effective image communication programs now require the formation of a partnership between the public relations professional and the institutional research staff. While it is the domain of the public relations professional to either directly communicate or assist others to communicate responses to critical publics, the organized research function at the college must assemble the data required to communicate to these publics. Moreover, the eventual measurement of critical publics' acceptance or reaction to these responses to key questions will also require the support of the institutional research office. In addition, researching perceptions of customer service calls for the involvement of research office professionals. On the other hand public relations personnel should be consulted in design of the questions which will be used for measuring communication to specific external publics.

Community college public relations professionals must have access to critical information detailing successful college outcomes that are related to the college's basic missions. Secondly, they must begin to systematically communicate such information.

Institutional effectiveness research has become much more common on community college campuses. Most regional accrediting agencies now require reports on student outcomes and educational achievements. While there are many nuances to community college mission based upon local application, public relations professionals may find it helpful to imagine what responses can be given to three of the very basic questions that could be asked of a community college. These questions relate to the three most common missions of transfer, career education and remedial education:

- If transfer is part of a college's mission, what is its transfer rate, and how successful are its students once they transfer?

- If career education is part of a college's mission, how many students obtain jobs in areas in which they were trained and are employers satisfied with the "products" of the college?

- If remedial education is part of a college's mission, how many students are eventually successful at "college-level work?"

Obviously there are many refinements of these questions that key publics generally ask concerning these basic missions. Yet, these simple questions are what legislative, public funding agencies and foundation givers are really asking.

A recent publication (1990) of the League for Innovation in the Community College, entitled, *Assessing Institutional Effectiveness in Community Colleges*, provides a list of 69 key questions related to the basic missions of a community college and the nature of the data gathering involved for each question. Public relations professionals should familiarize themselves with the nature of the questions raised in institutional effectiveness reporting and the data that would be available from these sources.

The PR Role in Communicating Research Findings

While a large number of effectiveness indicators may be required and utilized for internal institutional improvements, a careful review of all indicators must be undertaken to determine which should be chosen to clearly communicate the effectiveness of the community college to the key publics. That is, the image of the community college will be affected by the messages it regularly communicates. Public relations professionals must participate with key institutional administrators, such as the president, to determine which research on effectiveness should be highlighted and targeted toward which key publics.

The public relations professional has a responsibility to determine if these effectiveness "indicators" are clear and fair measures to communicate a "successful image" for the college. For example, does the transfer rate used by a college communicate clearly how many of its students transfer from the institution out of a pool of those who "intended" to transfer or whose academic preparation actually involved transfer courses? It would not, therefore, be appropriate to utilize a transfer rate that placed all students at an institution into a single pot (the denominator of the transfer rate), since many students who attend community colleges have no intention of transferring to a four-year college. General communication of a successful image of your transfer function could well be undermined if inappropriate measures are used.

Image communicators, rather than researchers, must become the consulted professionals on decisions involving the public use of effectiveness research. Once again, involvement in the front end at the design stage will be desirable if such research is to be used to enhance image.

Methods of Researching the Institutional Image

Beyond communicating positive answers based upon institutional research to questions of institutional quality, public relations professionals are concerned with the bottom line question of whether key publics have a favorable impression of the college. "Image" research is aimed at determining whether this has been achieved and whether the college has moved a key public toward a more favorable impression of the college.

Image research to determine the impression that a person has of a college falls into a number of broad categories. The first category of research relies solely upon responses without pre-prompting of possible "qualities" of the college. The second type of research suggests "image characteristics" and asks a person to react to them. The second type of research can range from a relatively informal approach to sophisticated survey techniques.

Unstructured Individual Interviews

A very common form of non-prompted research is the unstructured individual interview. Whether it is actually understood as such, one-on-one interviews with "key" or representative persons of a target public is a primary method of image information gathering. Since it is very open-ended, it may well lead to some new insights concerning the college's image. However, since many people may have a hard time articulating their impressions, this type of research is difficult to carry out and is often influenced by the interviewer.

Still, such interviews may well identify characteristics or attributes that a researcher will want to use in more structured research formats. In fact, since most interviewers have some pre-determined categories to explore in the interview, the purely unstructured interview may well be quite rare.

Structured Interviewing: Individual and Group

In either an individual format or in a small group setting, such as a focus group, a more productive image research tool will involve, at least, broad structuring of an interview. The broad missions of a community college, such as transfer, career preparation, job-retraining, basic skills, remedial, or continuing education could be used to ask the individual or group to determine the college's overall performance, or perhaps only one of these will be chosen to allow a more complete exploration. The interviewer may find it helpful to review the types of issues covered in the institutional effectiveness reports on community colleges to identify topics for discussion. Once again the League for Innovation publication (1990) could be used to develop such a list.

The interview should attempt to establish both an awareness of the college and knowledge of its performance levels. Sometimes, it is as important to determine that a key public has little awareness of the college or the college's role concerning a particular function (and therefore no image) as it is to determine that it has a "poor" image.

A more formal type of group interviewing is known as the focus group approach. While this approach may prove less useful for interviewing some very key influentials, the approach can be used successfully in image research aimed at enrollment analysis

A limited list of guidelines (Higginbotham and Cox, 1976) should be followed by those engaged in focus group interviewing in image research. First, focus group research is small group research. That is, "image" focus groups should be composed of approximately six to eight interviewees. While it is common to conduct focus group sessions with up to 12 participants, the "influentials" required to be gathered for "image" research may practically be more likely to occur in slightly smaller groups. Yet, the guidelines suggest that too few group interviewees may create too much pressure on each individual and limit honest responses, while too many interviewees reduce participation in the discussion by individual members. The suggested length of a focus group session is approximately ninety minutes to two hours, conducted in comfortable, pleasant surroundings.

Since the objective is to gather attitude information from the participants, the information gathered must be recorded. This can be done either through note taking or by tape. The interviewer should tell the participants which approach is being followed and explain why the information is being gathered.

The approach taken by the focus group leader is obviously the critical factor in successfully undertaking focus groups. The goal is to encourage a "guided" discussion on the topic, but a discussion characterized as "free and easy" in the minds of the participants. The group leader role should be filled by someone who is knowledgeable about the area, who can be both a good listener, yet a conversational prompter. Many individuals, frequently with counseling backgrounds, can lead these sessions.

Rather than attempting to quantify precisely the extent to which specific opinions are held by a key public, focus group analyses are used to identify themes and to develop insights into held opinions. It is important in such analysis not to give excessive weight to the more articulate members of a focus group. Moreover, since it is possible to have an atypical group, more than one focus group should be conducted on any particular topic.

Impression Rankings and Rating Systems

Kotler (1975) suggests two general types of image research that depend upon individuals reacting to lists of attributes of an organization—reputational profiles and semantic differentials. A closely related category of image research utilizes a technique known as Likert scales (Suskie, 1992). These research methods are considered "quantitative" rather than qualitative research and frequently utilize survey techniques including mailed questionnaires or phone interviews. In contrast with qualitative research methods, such as focus group interviewing, the intention of "quantitative research" is to provide measurement of the "image" impression that key publics hold of the college.

In *Reputational Profiles*, a person is asked to choose from a list of statements the ones that best fit their idea or impression of the entity in question. Frequently, the person is asked to rank order the list. The statements that are pre-selected are those most commonly made of such organizations. Since the quality of information collected may well suffer with long profile rankings, a reputational list of qualities should generally be limited to ten.

One variation to this type of research seeks to identify "key qualities." Respondents would be asked, for example, which three of ten statements are most generally true of the community college or a particular function of the college. The research is summarized and ranked in order of identified frequency of "key qualities."

Semantic Differentials, another form of impression rankings, suggest a series of adjective opposites that allow the respondent to rate an institution on a continuum of qualities. This type of research can be helpful in image research because it can provide clear contrasts of opinions. Moreover, the statistical properties of this kind of data allow for more sophisticated analysis than do the properties of simple ranking scales.

Likert Scales are perhaps the best known rating scales and require the respondent to rate items on a five point scale ranging, for example, from (1) strongly agree to (5) strongly disagree. Likert scales allow the gathering of a great deal of information concerning attitudes and opinion about particular subjects and are frequently used in "image" research.

The middle rank on a Likert ranking scale usually allows for a "not sure," "undecided" or "don't know" response and, therefore, does not force an opinion. Sometimes this provides people with a way out of expressing an opinion on a particular item. Frequently this column is checked off by respondents who are "unaware." In image research it is probably preferable to allow such a response rather than forcing an opinion from someone who may not really have sufficient knowledge of the topic.

Likert scale research can also be carried out in such a manner as to allow comparisons between how the respondent believes things "are," and how they believe things "should be." This type of research asks the same question twice, allowing the respondent to provide two opinions. The data provided from determining the size of the gap between what "is" and "should be" is exceptionally helpful in image research of key publics.

Likert scales research is the most frequent form of commercially available survey research tools. Community colleges considering image research should incorporate a mix of home-grown and purchased survey tools. Instruments such as the Community College Goals Inventory (CCGI) of the Educational Testing Service utilize the dual comparison Likert scale approach to determine the extent that basic community college goals are being met and the gap between the current achievement and a preferred status. The CCGI has frequently been used in preparation for accreditation self-studies. The instrument can also be utilized with external publics. There have also been examples, such as in Arizona, of the use of Likert scales to measure public opinion and image among key publics in entire states (Richardson and Doucette, 1982).

On the other hand, quick reaction "image research," measuring "first impression" or customer service of a college as required by Total Quality Management (TQM) analyses, frequently uses in-house surveys. Macomb Community College, for example, utilizes an "ABC" grading system to allow student users and the public to evaluate a list of services of the college.

Suskie (1992) suggests that letter grading (ABC) is an excellent approach for educational institutions to use. Many key publics are more than willing to "give a college a grade" on a number of critical factors. Such "satisfaction" grading systems are not only well understood by the general public but provide data that allows relatively sophisticated analyses.

Conclusion

The projection of a positive image for any community college will be significantly assisted by proper communication of institutional research and the use of research to provide precise measurement of key public reaction to the college. It is no longer possible for the public relations professional to sit along the sidelines when research with image communication potential is undertaken at the college. Public relations professionals have a responsibility to become partners with the research office in the communication of outcomes information concerning the college. Community college trustees and presidents need to challenge their public relations staffs to consider the "image" implications of outcomes data. Community college leaders need to be able to receive advice from such professionals on how best to use such data with the key publics or constituencies of the college.

REFERENCES

Alfred, Richard and Julie Weissman. *Higher Education and the Public Trust: Improving Stature in Colleges and Universities.* Washington, D.C.: Association for the Study of Higher Education, 1987.

Assessing Institutional Effectiveness in Community Colleges. Laguna Hills, California: League for Innovation, 1990.

Clark, Burton R. "The 'Cooling Out' Function Revisited." In *Questioning the Community College Role, New Directions for Community College 32.* Edited by George B. Vaughan. San Francisco: Jossey-Bass Publishers, 1980

Deegan, William L., and Tillery, Dale, ed. *Renewing the American Community College.* San Francisco: Jossey-Bass Publishers, 1985.

Higginbotham, James B. and Keith K. Cox. "Focus Group Interviews: A Reader." In *Qualitative Research in Marketing.* Edited by Danny N. Bellenger, Kenneth L. Bernhardt, and Jac L. Goldstucker. Chicago: American Marketing Association, 1976, pp. 7-28.

Kotler, Philip. *Marketing for Nonprofit Organizations.* New Jersey: Prentice-Hall, Inc., 1975.

Richardson, R. C., Jr., Doucette, D. S., & Armenta, R. R. *Missions of Arizona Community Colleges.* Tempe: Arizona State University, 1982.

Suskie, Linda A. *Questionnaire Survey Research: What Works.* Tallahassee, Fla: Association for Institutional Research, 1992.

Zwerling, L, S. *Second Best: The Crisis of the Community College.* New York: McGraw-Hill Book Company, 1976.

Finding –and Hearing–Your Constituents

Rio Hondo College was built in the mid-1960s for 5,000 mostly Caucasian, middle-class students from a midsized community in Southern California. As the community grew, adjacent cities were added to the district and the demographics changed. The student population reflected that growth and change. Almost three decades later, student population neared 15,000. Knowing the market was imperative to intelligent management and college growth. The acknowledged paradigm was that the college enjoyed a good standing in the community. There were perceptions but no hard baseline of information on which to plan.

In 1989 a College Development Plan was initiated through a Title III grant. The first step was a Gallup study for a sense of how the college was viewed from the outside. Phone interviews were conducted with 535 randomly selected adult heads of households (40 in Spanish), 229 service area high school juniors and seniors, 210 parents, 53 high school guidance counselors and 53 high school teachers. Results showed that most held "good" perceptions about the college, saw few "outstanding" features and perceived few lacked services. We had no real market niche among our competitors and some old stereotypes still lingered. It was also apparent that in addition to the traditional service populations, there were new, growing populations of college students and potential college students about which and from whom more information was needed.

The next step was a series of focus groups conducted by Kumamoto Associates, specialists in multicultural/multilingual community needs assessments. In 1991, a mailing of 1,000 bilingual notices to individuals and community groups invited them to community meetings. Reminder postcards, follow-up calls to key individuals and groups along with publicity in the schools and on television and radio set the stage for the forums. A majority of attendees were not the traditional Rio Hondo College service population; about half were Spanish speaking. They were animated and vocal, voicing the feelings and concerns of their neighborhoods as well as personal opinions.

Key findings indicated that the Rio Hondo community was very diverse, with many needs and expectations. Bilingualism, child care, career training, night classes, outreach programs and access were main issues. These two studies and their road signs for future directions now play a significant role in planning and implementation. They have been used in the college accreditation process, in staff and faculty education, in establishing an Image and marketing program, and in developing the college's long-range plan. For example, the studies were used to update and standardize marketing strategies for the nursing program, transforming an underenrolled program into a thriving one.

Rio now has its baseline data. However, neither our populations nor our responses are static. Like California and the community college, our student body will change and we will need to continue to adapt. Part of the long-range plan is to keep our finger on the pulse of our district and use the accumulating data to track our progress and as a compass to navigate the rough community college seas in California in the next decade.

by Beth Fernandez, Public Information and Alumni Officer
Rio Hondo College
Whitter, California

Functional Focus Groups

How are we doing? Chemeketa Community College in Salem, Oregon, has found a relatively quick and easy way to find out and keep monitoring their systems.

The college regularly conducts focus groups on programs, publications and procedures to assess student, staff and community satisfaction and to gain input before major projects are undertaken. Focus groups are comprised of anywhere from ten to 15 people who are representative of a particular college or district population. In an informal but facilitated 70-minute meeting, focus group participants are asked open-ended questions that gauge their level of satisfaction and encourage the sharing of ideas.

A couple of things happen with focus groups, according to Alan Koch, Chemeketa's Director of Marketing, Publications and Student Life. "You get direct feedback, and the act of going through the process makes you a much better listener," he says. "It makes you that much more mindful of what your customer wants." For example, students noted that the college coffee shop wasn't open late enough to serve evening students; now it is open later at night.

Koch estimates that he has conducted about 60 focus groups in the last three years on everything from food services to community perception of the college. In addition to assessing satisfaction, focus groups help the college identify priorities, both within specific programs and for the institution as a whole.

Chemeketa has also gained valuable input from business people. Employers in the college's district not only told the institution what they appreciated about graduates, but also what additional skills they want their employees to have.

With regard to publications, focus groups are useful for

both pre-testing and post-testing. A focus group held to review the design of the statewide community college viewbook prior to its publication resulted in changes. Chemeketa's catalog and class schedule have also seen changes as a result of post-publication focus groups.

Just when to conduct a focus group depends upon individual need, but Chemeketa has found it best to invest the effort before any major change in policy is initiated. "Do one whenever you find yourself at a key decision-making point," says Koch.

by Kim Christiansen
Publications Specialist
Chemeketa Community College
Salem, Oregon

Using Research to Hire Administrators

Too often, colleges plan initiatives or hire new administrators without first testing for image or direction. St. Louis Community College recently hired a new chancellor and has begun a major reorganization of its administrative structure. Before job descriptions were written or advertisements designed, the college sponsored focus groups with internal as well as external audiences. Discussion focused on the mission of the college, its role in the community, new initiatives and challenges, and the type of leadership needed to achieve results.

Feedback from meetings was used as a foundation for developing leadership expectations for the chancellor. It also indicated areas of concern and gave a picture of the type of leadership most suited for the challenges ahead. Too often in times of change, we focus on internal needs without adequately taking into account the greater community we serve; discussion with members of the community added the dimension of community expectations to internal concerns.

The focus groups were coordinated through the college's research office with staff members serving as facilitators. Transcripts of the collected data were compiled and used to create the job description for the chancellor, shared with the board of trustees and the campus community, and employed in departmental goal setting. The cost was small, but the effort reaped big returns.

by Ann Brand
Community Relations Director
St. Louis Community College at Florissant Valley
St. Louis, Missouri

Testing the Vote

In a state where colleges depend not only on the benevolence of the legislature, but on the direct support of the citizenry, the failure of a bond issue can kill a budget and an image, too. In the summer of 1991, trustees from Portland Community College in Oregon authorized a comprehensive study of the college's performance.

The purpose of the study was to give the board an objective look at how well the community felt the college was meeting its needs, to assess areas of weakness, and to determine how best to allocate resources in the years ahead. Residents and students were surveyed by telephone, all full-time faculty and staff were surveyed by mail, and in-depth interviews were conducted with key community leaders representing business, labor, social service agencies, employers, churches, other educational institutions, and minority groups.

The results held many rewards and a few surprises. Members of the public and the students were overwhelmingly positive about PCC, the major reason being personal experience. Close to two-thirds (63 percent) reported that they or someone in their household had taken a class at the college. While internally some concern was expressed about Portland's mission being too broad, students and the public saw diverse programming as one of the college's most positive qualities. The most significant communications need appeared to be internal, with staff and faculty rating the college less highly than the general public. The public did not have a clear idea of college financing, indicating a need for further education, but felt the state should pay a larger share of operational costs.

On top of the other positive perceptions about PCC, members of the public indicated they were open to requests

for funding, showing that a bond issue might be successful.
The subsequent bond issue pastsed the next May with a 10
percent margin.

by Norma Jean Germond
Trustee
Portland Community College
Portland, Oregon

CHAPTER 3

Reaping Community Trust

by Starnell K. Williams
Associate Vice President for Communications
Midlands Technical College

About the Author

Starnell Williams

    Starnell K. Williams, Associate Vice President for Communications at Midlands Technical College, began her career in corporate marketing and advertising. She holds a master's degree in higher education administration for the University of South Carolina where she is a doctoral candidate. Ms. Williams is a graduate of the Harvard University Institute for the Management of Lifelong Education and was honored as the 1990 Administrator of the Year by the South Carolina Technical Education Association. Under her leadership, her college has garnered numerous regional and national marketing awards and has experienced a more than 60 percent enrollment growth over the last five years.

*T*wenty years ago, marketing had an undeserved negative image among many academicians. It simply was not traditional to "market" education. Marketing was a corporate concept, replete with promotional gimmickry at its worst. But because of their very nature, community colleges had to serve populations so diverse and scattered, that nontraditional methods of reaching students had to be developed and implemented. And with that, community colleges entered a new era.

It's been a long time since skeptical budget officers first grudgingly allocated a few dollars of community college money into a new line item called marketing. But marketing appeared to offer the best hope that loose, poorly defined institutional images could be solidified to attract new students. Acting on that premise, community colleges began to intentionally position their institutional identity in the marketplace. They purposefully became more image conscious.

Marketing, in its purest form, simply means getting a useful product to consumers. In higher education, marketing can be used to increase student (consumer) awareness of the product (programs and services) and to enhance the image of the institution. Both functions have financial objectives: to increase enrollment in the immediate future and to create a public trust that will maintain enrollments and resources in the long run. (Jones, 1989).

Marketing became an important part of not only attracting students, but also redefining the college's relationship to the community. Organizations such as the National Council for Marketing and Public Relations (NCMPR), formerly the National Council for Community Relations, changed their names to add *marketing*. Colleges restructured, became customer-oriented and began to focus more attention and resources on image campaigns.

Over the last decade, a spreading acceptance of the need to market community colleges found its way into the mainstream of strategic plans and administrative structures. By the late 1980s, hardly a community college existed without a marketing element (O'Banion, 1989). It seemed that marketing was not only a good idea, as was first thought, but instrumental to meeting the uncertainty of the future. Image building and marketing became essential for community colleges trying to keep pace with a changing environment (Golden, 1991). Market-oriented approaches presented a unique opportunity to embrace student diversity and did much to include, rather than polarize, special populations. By exploring the relationship of colleges and the people they served, institutions began to gain a more complete understanding of the increasingly crowded and competitive educational marketplace.

Along with widespread success have come questions about the future of community college marketing. Indeed, institutions now need to sharpen and control their newfound marketing abilities. The time has come to view the future of community college marketing in the context of institutional accountability and image preservation.

In an era of restructuring and downsizing that is sweeping the corporate world with faddish consistency, colleges should consider marketing just as essential to their mission as they do quality instruction. Even in the cost-cutting climate that led General Motors to slice its professional workforce, a primary goal of that corporate giant remained to sell quality cars. In a situation where the cost of obtaining a college education has escalated dramatically, it is essential for the student/customer to understand the value of the educational product and have faith that it will be worth the fee. Particularly as institutions face further tuition increases, maintaining the trust of the people is crucial. The image of the community college, its perceived values and benefits, has to become central to its growth and development.

Marketing and Community Trust

Usually when a product goes to market, there is a shared knowledge of the value expected in return for the purchase price. The marketing of education differs from the marketing of many consumer-based products because the public does not always know what to expect after the sale. This situation of a symmetrical information exchange between the buyer and the seller is called a trust market (Winston, 1992). In educational marketing, product refers not only to goods, but to services as well. It must also deal with perceived needs versus the real needs of the customers. The principal product of community colleges is quality education that can be applied to a career or as a step toward an advanced degree. However, the definition of what quality is and the value of the difference the product will make in the buyer's life may remain a mystery in the pre-enrollment phase of the transaction.

Operating in a trust market, the institution accepts the obligation to honestly estimate the worth of the product in relation to the benefits that the customer may expect. Colleges have an excellent idea of the product being offered, but there is a large element of dependency on community trust when marketing the institution. Certainly in a market built on trust, any lack of public confidence must be a major concern.

The Council for the Advancement and Support of Education (CASE) recognizes this trust problem in its *Revised Strategic Plan* (1992). The document states in part:

> The public perception of education, and especially educational institutions, will not improve and may well deteriorate further. In addition to issues of cost and quality, there will be questions about the direction, or lack of it, of our institutions and their ability to change to meet evolving educational needs.

That certainly sounds like an image problem that must be addressed through marketing. In fact, American education is currently facing a decline in public trust that is unprecedented in its history. The people are demanding answers to some difficult questions about cost, quality, institutional effectiveness and outcomes. Institutions generally ignore the questions and only sporadically provide any answers (Levine, 1992). The intrinsic value of the college emanates from the quality of its programs and services, no doubt. However, without strong publicly accepted reputations, community colleges will not be very competitive.

Speaking about competitiveness, Calvin Coolidge once said, "The business of America is business." An updated version of that statement, according to the *Kiplinger Washington Letter*, is "The business of America is education." (Kiplinger, 1989). And the business of education, like the national economy, is cyclical. Many factors combine to determine whether the demand for the college's product is up or down.

Changing demographics, advances in technology and the increasing demand for creative educational options stand as contradictions to diminishing college budgets and tough economic conditions for consumers. It is now time to concentrate on preserving marketshare and re-examining the match between the community college's mission and image. Now is not a good time to abandon what has been accomplished. Community colleges simply can't afford to isolate themselves from their markets.

That's why marketing is a perpetual process. To create a successful image program, reap the rewards of community trust and confidence, and then forget its principles is like spending months developing a comprehensive policy manual, placing it on the shelf, and then never looking at it again. It simply would not be a wise investment of time and resources. People must be assured of multiple returns on their investment. More than ever, the public needs to know why they should trust the college in their community. The terms may differ — reputation, quality, dignity, effectiveness, status — but what is implied is the need to assure the public that they will get what they pay for (Winston, 1992), and more.

Shared Responsibilities

The Education Commission of the States declared in its 1990 report *A Vision for American Education:*

Education must affirm the shared responsibilities of all stakeholders in the educational enterprise — students, faculty, administrators, board members, policy makers, education leaders, business and community organizations and the community at large.

The strength of a college's image stems from the values held within the institution. This internal tone must be of sufficient intensity to foster the trust of the college's external audience. Colleges need to persuade the public, but must first believe themselves, that the quality of education is a priority second to none (Bok, 1992).

Marketing is directly involved in aligning this vision with reality. It consolidates responsibilities with multiple components and participants. Commitment, especially long-term commitment, thrives best when it produces results. Commitment to a marketing philosophy asks that long-term goals to optimize customer satisfaction be achieved through the participation of all who belong to the college family. To be successful at producing results, the marketing mandate must come from the highest levels of the organization.

A college's governing body should be foremost in understanding the importance of institutional image as a part of an interactive relationship with the community. With the help and understanding of its trustees, the college is better able to secure the commitment of legislative, business and civic leadership.

With the support of its trustees, the president chooses the college's pathway toward fulfilling its mission. It is also the president who must organize and empower the college's staff to mobilize the institution toward effectiveness and a positive public image. When support for image enhancement begins with the executive arm of the college, it is possible to enlist the entire college family as practitioners of a market-oriented philosophy. Armed with the support of the president and a deserved collegiate reputation, marketing can better impact the institution's image in the community.

Faculty members are critically important to marketing specific academic programs. Through a coordinated effort, the academic and technical units of the community college can deliver messages about individual departments and actively explain the college's programs and services to the community.   College staff members should understand they are representing their college as they interact with students and the community-at-large. Individual staff members encountered by students and prospective students, alumni, or donors are the personification of the college and greatly influence the perceived image.

Students are perhaps the best marketing resource the college can tap. Students who feel strongly about the benefits they receive from the college may be organized as student ambassadors or peer mentors to share their experiences with others. Because community college students are so diverse in their backgrounds, specialized groups can be enlisted to tailor the college's message throughout the community.

The college's alumni are an excellent resource. Alumni serve as college supporters in publications and college literature. Their testimonials and success stories are powerful evidence the college delivered on its promises.

The active support of community leaders reaffirms the positive relationship the college has with business and industry. Through service on the college's foundation board or similar board of visitors, leaders outside the institution are trustworthy image amplifiers.

Trustees, administrators, faculty, students, alumni, and community leaders all have significant roles in the development and enhancement of the community college image. The importance of each of these groups must not be underestimated.

Creating a Functional Structure for Building Trust

When community college marketing was a relatively new concept, almost everyone thought it meant advertising. Today marketing seems to embrace as many aspects as there are institutions that practice it. But those institutions that are best at marketing have found a synergy of purpose among functional areas which span the roll-call of customer services. Those community colleges that boldly group diverse areas such as recruiting, media relations, publications, student information and advertising have expanded their service orientations to include Total Quality Management and other efficiency methods. But all of these service-based practices have been designed to promote effectiveness through problem solving throughout the community college. After nearly a decade of restructuring, many college marketing units can scarcely recall their original nomenclature when they were separate, perhaps turf-protective, and ineffectively scattered in their efforts to serve students and define an institution to its public.

Yet the specialized skills remain even if the broader activities are now more centralized. And it is not important that every college uses the same terms to describe what marketing people do. What is important is the culture of the organization that values the need to communicate with the people it serves. Marketing's objective is to facilitate communication by establishing a two-way conversation with the community, perhaps the best way to earn the public trust.

Community colleges should organize resources in a systematic way to ensure all elements and individuals necessary to marketing can interact to foster an institutional attitude in which to thrive (Golden, 1991). Having marketing as a unit function is an investment in maintaining public trust. It provides the college with a window through which information can pass to and from the community. There is no one prescription for accomplishing this task, but many colleges feel a traditional corporate model of marketing is the best way to interact in the global 1990s (Williams, *in press*).

According to this systematic structure, a marketing team is assembled with the leadership of skilled professionals who have the experience and judgment to allocate resources for the most effective and controlled marketing approach. Principle responsibilities include building a corporate identity and managing the myriad of activities and opportunities for image building.

For best results, marketing decision makers should report to the CEO, as they do in the business world. Community college presidents are realizing that the marketing function cannot operate as a separate entity, adjunct to the rest of the campus. Marketing must be a part of the mainstream of college life, an integral part of the whole, able to give support to the whole institution. It has become a major administrative function in its own right, and the way a president organizes the marketing function is critical to the success, and image, of the college (Jones, 1992).   This positioning ensures the direct translation of leadership strategies into action, closely connecting the marketing viewpoint to the administrative decision-making focus of the college.

Each college must clearly identify and articulate the marketing goals it desires to accomplish and methodically move toward achieving them.   Size and resources differ widely in the nation's more than 1,200 two-year institutions, but it is always prudent to understand exactly why any particular element of a marketing plan is being used and what the specific outcome should be.   Costly mistakes can result from continuing to perform routine tasks without periodically re-thinking the purpose of each.   It doesn't matter how many ads are purchased or how many brochures are printed.   All that counts is what works for each college and its community.

Regardless of the image building activities chosen, it is impera-tive for the college to continually evaluate its own changing market and utilize deftness and control over the array of marketing strate-gies available.   It is essential to target goals and determine what course of action will make the most difference in shaping and re-shaping the college's image.

Global Emphasis vs. Local Needs — A Trust Issue

A large measure of community trust centers on product cred-ibility.   A college must offer relevant programs that the community needs.   As community colleges seek greater public understanding of their mission, inevitably the question is broached whether local needs supersede global relevance.   Local constituencies often confine their expectations of the community college to an intro-verted perspective that the college should only train students for existing local jobs.   Such a posture does not satisfy the avowed mission of the community college to prepare citizens for the future.   Simply put, community colleges must increase public awareness about the education required to compete in a global economy.

Community colleges are complex organizations, greatly influenced by changes in technology and market needs. Colleges must monitor external trends to improve their long-term responsiveness to those changing needs. Students return to the open marketplace after graduation and must take with them enough added value to provide them with lifetime benefits (Lapin, 1992). The world awaits. And the world no longer includes just the local and regional economy as often perceived by the constituents of most community colleges. The key to America's economic future is how well the quality of the nation's workforce can be improved (Brock, 1991).

Preparing students to work in a national or global economic market does not mean neglecting the needs of business and industry in the college's immediate service area. Rather, it means responding to the fact that companies in the service area have already concluded they must be competitive in the worldwide marketplace. There is no longer such a thing as a "locally" relevant education. The shelf-life of limited training is quite short indeed and market trust is quickly lost when low product value is perceived.

In *Megatrends 2000*, Naisbett and Aburdene forecast:

- The primary challenge...in the 1990s is to encourage the new, better-educated worker to be more entrepreneurial, self-managing and oriented toward life-long learning,
- The labor supply will increase less than 1percent a year, the slowest growth since the 1930s,
- Corporations will have to recruit people who did not work in the 1980s.
- Women will take two-thirds of the new jobs created in the 1990s (Naisbitt, 1989).

Community colleges are in a unique position to address these major workforce challenges. The under-educated, the unemployed, women and minorities illustrative of the changing trends in workplace demographics are the same cast assembled at the doorway of local community colleges seeking the enabling knowledge to become world-class workers.

Local patterns in the economy speak volumes about the need to embrace global thinking. If, for example, a college experiences a declining demand for graduates enrolled in industrial and engineering technologies, it would be prudent to assess the manufacturing sector's changing needs. If manufacturing is to return to the American economy at the volume it once experienced, it will be knowledge-intensive rather than labor-intensive (Cappo, 1990).

Community colleges need to be the first to respond to the current and future environment and provide clear information about how the college can be of value to the individual and the community. It is not a case of replacing local needs with international objectives. The local community has to be prepared for worldwide competition.

Marketing must include a recognition of the needs of present and future students, as well as community and business needs. It should be integral to the development of an educational product to meet those needs. This responsibility includes recommendations on curriculum development and scheduling options that respond to previously identified market needs. Essential to successful image enhancement and public trust are providing courses and packaging delivery timeframes that people want to buy. Henry Ford thought everyone wanted a black car until other auto makers started producing automobiles in a variety of colors. The best marketing advice is to ask the customer how to improve any product, even educational programming.

The community college marketing function is responsible for providing awareness of available choices and translating information collected through accountability studies into a consistency that can be absorbed and understood by the public. In this resolve, institutional effectiveness data can be powerful image-building tools. While marketing cannot create the product, in a large measure it is the caretaker of the institution's credibility.

To accomplish widespread understanding, marketing must operate on a tiered system of information exchange. Versions of institutional information should be targeted to reach different levels of the community. The local aspect of image enhancement should revolve around how the college is of value to the people who live and work in the area. It also influences the amount of foundation or private support the local community will contribute to the college.

On a statewide level, the marketing message must translate into how funding allocated to higher education positively affects economic development. Nationally, there is the responsibility to support the reputation of the college as part of the system of two-year post-secondary institutions, and internationally the image may attract foreign investment to the local area. Multi-level communication provides a mechanism for grouping image concerns and ultimately focusing on community needs. Colleges can't simply claim to be on top of new market trends. They have to demonstrate a responsiveness to documented needs by letting the community know what they are currently doing well and what to expect from the college in the future.

Image Enhancement Is A Wise Investment

When monetary investment is involved, the concept of trust is paramount. Colleges ask for public and private dollars from their communities through tuition and auxiliary support. They in turn must prove themselves trustworthy through the best use of institutional funds.

In some parts of the country, community colleges have experienced so much growth and demand for services that enrollments have been capped and waiting lists exist for popular programs. At other colleges, funding levels are insufficient to meet demands for new programs and services. Given such constraints, is it time for community colleges to stop recruiting students? Can dollars spent on image enhancement be justified in tight college budgets? These are serious questions that should not intimidate institutional leaders. They are valid issues that need to be examined in light of the future and not the past.

If a college is operating at capacity, it shouldn't concentrate its marketing strictly on recruiting activities. Colleges that view marketing as simply getting as many students as possible misunderstand the concept and may perform a disservice to their communities. Such production driven models are not the best use of marketing abilities.

Colleges should be concerned about their images because they believe in providing opportunities that need to be understood by potential students, employers, and funding agencies alike. Full enrollment leaves no room for abandoning image concerns. The need to preserve a quality image includes retaining marketshare, but should also speak to the need of institutional growth and improvement. Colleges that have marketed well, cared about their reputations in their community, and grown to full capacity must continue to be image conscious. To do otherwise is to invite declines in enrollment and reputations that eventually follow a period of inattention to promoting community understanding.

Expensive is a difficult term to apply to image campaigns when they often serve as the visual value statements representing the college to the community. *Invaluable* would perhaps be more correct when describing the worth of supporting and enhancing the college's credibility and fostering the goodwill of the community. The college's image can't be taken for granted.   It is the responsibility of the board of trustees, the president, and the college's marketing unit to enhance and communicate the integrity of the institution's public perception. College marketing efforts must continually broadcast the institution's benefits and strengths. If there is any doubt about the worth of image-related expenditures, the substitution of the term *reputation* should clarify what is really being transmitted to the community. Old time corporate marketing legends Coke, Xerox, and Campbell's Soup are still investing heavily in image-oriented messages, even though virtually everyone is familiar with their products.

Not only does a positive community perception reproduce a student body each term, it also impacts funding levels. Enlightened resource management leaders remember that public funding for colleges is tied to student enrollment and solicitation of private support begins with a trusted institutional reputation. As the public demands more detailed information about the colleges they pay for and support, it is difficult to imagine not devoting attention and resources to the college's reputation by protecting and enhancing institutional credibility.

The Future

As our community colleges promote quality through excellence in teaching and service to students and as they focus more closely on institutional effectiveness, they can reap a harvest of community trust. In the future, community college marketing efforts will be increasingly tied to accountability issues and will be critical to attaining advocacy for the college.

The future will provide opportunities and challenges for community colleges and their students as social and economic change agents in a world itself changing at an unmatched pace.

In such times of transformation, it is fundamental that our community colleges keep reliable communication channels open to numerous constituencies. It's a question of trust.

REFERENCES

Bok, D.   Reclaiming the public trust. *Change.* July-August, 1992.

Brock, W. E.   Continuous training for the high-skilled workforce. *Community, Technical and Junior College Journal.* Vol. 61, no. 4, 1992.

Cappo, J.   *Future Scope,* Longman Financial Services Publishing, 1990.

Golden, S.   Sweat the small stuff and you'll come out ahead: marketing that makes a difference. *Community, Technical and Junior College Journal:* Vol. 61, no. 4, 1991.

Jones, S. W.   Marketing and retention in enrollment management, In Ryan (Ed.), *Marketing and Development for Community Colleges,* Council for the Advancement and Support of Education, Washington, D.C.,1989.

Jones, S. W.   College Advancement: The hottest game in town, *NCMPR Counsel,* 1992.

Kiplinger, A. H. & K. A. Kiplinger .   *America in the Global 90s.* Washington, D.C. The Kiplinger Washington Editors, Inc., 1991.

Lapin, J. D.   Back to the future: anticipating and preparing for change. *AACJC Journal.* Vol. 63, no. 1, 1992.

Levine, A.   Why colleges are continuing to lose the public trust. *Change.* July-August, 1992.

Naisbitt. J. & P. Aburdene .   *Megatrends 2000: Ten New Directions for   the 1990s.* New York: William Morrow and Company, Inc. , 1989.

O'Banion, T.   *Innovation in the Community College.* New York: Macmillan Publishing Co., 1989.

Williams, S. K. (*in press*) .   Marketing the vision.   In G. A. Baker III (Ed) *Handbook on Community Colleges in America.*   West Port, CT: Greenwood Publishing Group.

Winston, G. C.   Hostility, maximization, & the public trust: economics and higher education.   *Change.*   July-August, 1992.

A President's Vision

When I became president of Midlands Technical College, I discovered a marketing gold mine — a college that was much better than the community perceived it to be. We faced a two-fold challenge: the internal perception of the college needed improvement as a prelude to communicating a strong image to the community.

To promote self-actualization, a strategic planning process was established that created a Vision for Excellence which described the kind of college the faculty and staff desired the institution to be. A strategic plan was developed to make that vision a reality. Marketing the college to the community was a critical component of that plan.

The college was reorganized to establish a marketing division which reported to the president. The division was designed to include all first contact services to students and community groups. We conducted a search for a marketing professional with experience in the private sector to fill the leadership role as founding director of the new unit. The Associate Vice President for Marketing also became a participant in policy-making decisions as part of the college's executive staff.

The college's marketing division was characterized by diverse groups which had previously been assigned to other divisions. It included recruiting staff, members of the existing development office and telecommunications personnel. Professional designers were added to fill a creative gap and insure total control of visual products. The resulting dynamic combination of experience and duties cross-referenced the tasks of communicating with student-customers and formulating community image enhancement tactics.

The new division soon developed a synergy of purpose

and a contagious spirit representative of TQM problem-solving groups. The goal was the restructuring of the college's image and community relationships. The principle focus of the resulting marketing plan has been the concise control of techniques and budgets to achieve optimum, measurable results.

The outcomes have been phenomenal. After the marketing division was established, enrollment growth exceeded 60 percent in the ensuing five-year period and the college grew to nearly 9,000 entering fall students. Community surveys indicate that the college's mission is understood by the general population and is valued at a 94 percent approval rating. Ties with economic development groups have been strengthened and the college's Foundation is enjoying unprecedented public support. This year, county governments provided full funding for the college in an environment which has seen dramatic cuts in government spending. A significant image success measure is the college's increased market share of college-bound high school graduates. Last fall the college enrolled more than 30 percent of area high school seniors attending any college, up from 15 percent five years ago. The college has been honored with numerous regional and national professional awards for marketing expertise.

In the five years the college has had a proactive marketing and image program, the community reputation of the institution has reached the level its quality educational programs deserve. The image of the college has been extremely important to establishing the institution as a first choice in higher education. An added benefit to students had been the examination of all customer-related intake services to insure ease of entry. Each time a new area of opportunity arises to strengthen the college's ability to communicate with its customers, the marketing division responds with an appropriate strategy.

For instance, an Office of Access and Equity was established two years ago to better communicate with and retain minority students. Another exemplary program, the Ambassa-dor Assembly, has been created in which honor students participate in a competitive selection process to represent the college in the community and serve as peer advisors. The Ambassadors and the college's executive staff held a workshop and roundtable meetings this year which provided meaningful student input into the on-going strategic planning process.

The bottom line is a college should never take its marketshare and community reputation for granted. It should be a continuing priority to tell the community about the accomplishments and effectiveness of the college and project institutional strengths to the public, the business community and funding agencies. As our college's true identity was communicated, the rewards have been priceless when measured against our commitment to serve students and contribute to the economic success of our community.

by Dr. James L. Hudgins
President
Midlands Technical College
Columbia, South Carolina

Rethink Phillips

A community-wide survey completed by outside consultants for Phillips County Community College in Helena, Arkansas, showed that there were four areas of misconception about our college. Since these needed to be addressed, the Advancement Office at Phillips implemented a *Rethink Phillips* campaign.

The four problems identified were concerns about 1) the transferability of PCCC courses, 2) whether or not the college provided state-of-the-art equipment, 3) the professionalism of our faculty compared to a four-year institution, and 4) the amount of our tuition. The advancement staff conducted research and borrowed ideas from NCMPR on how other colleges had handled these particular community college myths, and Rethink Phillips was born.

Our campaign goal was to consistently place the rebuttals to these four items in (and on) every format available to us. The Rethink campaign was first announced in the quarterly college newsletter, followed by bimonthly direct mail pieces, posters, billboards, luncheons, tours, and newspaper and radio advertising. The Rethink Phillips logo was incorporated into everything we did, from catalog covers to our booth at the county fair.

As a result of the campaign, we not only got our point across, but we now have a new vehicle for getting the word out. In the last Rethink newsletter, we included a reply card asking that it be returned by those who were willing to spread the word about good things at Phillips. The response was great, and we call this group our Phillips Affiliates. These new friends of the college have agreed to meet three times a year to hear about changes, special offerings, additions to the curriculum, faculty/staff/college honors, outstanding students and scholarship recipients and any other current college events. They have pledged to then take this information into the community and share it with their friends and acquaintances. Rethink Phillips not only helped us solve an image problem of the past, but it has also provided a means to combat—if not prevent—other image problems in the future.

by Betsy Huff, Director of College Advancement
Phillips County Community College
Helena, Arkansas

CHAPTER 4

Creating the Image Team

by Sandra Golden
Associate Vice President
for Public Affairs and Information
Cuyahoga Community College

About the Author

Sandra Golden

Sandra Golden is associate vice president for public affairs and information at Cuyahoga Community College in Ohio. She has more than 23 years of experience in marketing and public relations at CCC.

She is a past president of the National Council for Marketing and Public Relations (NCMPR), past president of the Greater Cleveland Chapter of the Public Relations Society of America, and is currently an international trustee of the Council for the Advancement and Support of Education (CASE), where she is chair of its Institutional Relations Commission.

Her work has been recognized with more than 70 professional awards and honors and she is a regularly sought after national speaker and regular contributor to professional journals.

A college's image sets the stage for how well a college is able to do its job. Perceptions, whether accurate or not, affect enrollment, finances and community support and linkages. While the public relations/marketing professional working under the overall leadership of the president and trustees is officially responsible for creating and communicating that image, the most effective institutions will have created various image teams from both within and outside the college.

A Shared Vision

These teams can contain various numbers of people, but as teams, they work toward a common objective to support the college.

The significance of the individuals on these teams is that they bring various perspectives to the table. Their input must first help shape directions and activities and then help carry the institution's message more broadly into the community. This broad-based perspective is what contributes to the value of our community colleges; and to make good decisions, we need to consider the views of many individuals inside and outside of the operation. To be most effective, our employees and supporters must see the total picture and share our vision of education and its impact on our society.

It is critical that the college has this overriding shared vision and that it speaks with one clear voice, whether the message comes from marketing, development, trustees, administrators, faculty, support staff, volunteers or others in the communication cycle. The message needs to be repeated consistently, regularly and proactively.

While what the public considers the image is not always based on total information and truth or on what we deserve to have the

public believe, we need to realize a number of factors. First,
perception can be reality. What people perceive influences how
they think and act in regard to your institution. On the other hand,
our image will be ultimately based on the reality of our quality —
the service and programs we offer and how well we do our education job. The first step in any realistic expectation of image
enhancement then has to be to put "our house in order," to evaluate what we do, and what we should do. Then we must concern
ourselves with what the perceptions are (internally and externally)
and how we can create the appropriate message and communicate it
effectively.

While most will agree theoretically with this description of
involvement resulting in shared vision, how do we really make this
happen in complex educational organizations relating to complex
communities? While the public relations/marketing staff are the
professionals with the expertise in developing strategy and using
the tools and technical skills in the areas of image, the critical issue
is how we take the important perspectives and resources of others
whose main responsibilities lie elsewhere and put them on the
Image Team as well.

Leadership Signals from the Trustees and President

The leadership of the president and the board sets the stage for
the climate and culture in which the institution functions. How
they feel and act will influence how others feel and act as well. To
create effective college images then, they must believe in the
significance of not only the institution and what it does, but in the
significance of the public relations/marketing function as a critical
part of enabling the institution to do what it needs to do. If this
belief is not already there, it becomes the responsibility of the
public relations/marketing professionals to call attention through
examples and demonstrate to presidents, and through them to
boards, the value of good PR and marketing and the significance of
a positive image to accomplishing institutional goals.

The actions, then, of presidents and boards can send signals of
their support in a number of ways, not only to the public relations

and marketing professionals, but to the entire institution with whom these professionals need to work, and can give them the flexibility and credibility to do what needs to be done to promote their colleges.

This empowerment should include authority, resources, involvement, recognition, and teamwork:

Authority: Clear authority and responsibility to the PR professional for decisions in this area should be delegated through formal college policies and procedures established by the Board. Assignments for leadership in overall strategy and direction of projects in public relations and marketing should be communicated by the president.

Resources: While all institutions have limited budgets, certain levels of resources are basic to accomplish what needs to be done in marketing and public relations. Budgeting allocations themselves send messages of priorities within the college. College marketing begins in the president's office. The president's commitment of resources must include trained professionals, adequate facilities and equipment, and a sufficient operating budget. Marketing can no longer operate on "what's left" of the budget after more important areas have been funded. It has attained a top priority status itself.

Involvement: The marketing function must be a part of the top level college team. Marketing professionals must have regular access to the college president. To be most effective, these professionals need to be involved when key college decisions are being discussed, at a point where they can advise and influence directions and point out image implications. This does not mean that presidents and trustees must shun hard decisions, but they need the counsel of those who can tell them how those decisions will be received publicly and suggest the best ways to communicate them. How and when college leaders communicate decisions and react to difficult situations is as important as the responses and decisions themselves.

Recognition: How community college presidents promote the responsibilities and accomplishments of their public relations and marketing areas is as important as how they organize and empower them. Presidents should recognize and reward outstanding performance and achievement by encouraging communications professionals to make presentations or be acknowledged at key meetings, at conventions and professional conferences, and at board meetings.

Teamwork: Trustees and presidents must serve with the communications professionals as the top leadership team for college image enhancement. Trustees, as representatives of the community, bring diverse viewpoints and information from the community to the college to carry out their responsibilities as policy setters. After decisions and messages are determined, trustees also serve as part of the leadership voice to take the message to external constituencies. To do so, they must be kept informed by college leadership so they can make good decisions and anticipate community responses.

The president is the most visible, out-front image-maker and spokesperson for the college. The president sets the tone and establishes the vision for the institution, and communicates internally and externally, from the planning stages to the followup stages of major college activities.

This leadership Image Team cannot function effectively in isolation, however, and will, in various circumstances, turn to an expanded number of individuals to form larger image teams. These broader-based teams are usually involved when colleges evaluate their missions, when they develop and implement marketing plans, and when they must gain support from the community-at-large.

Defining the Mission

Basic to any institution's operation and image is its mission statement. While many community colleges will have some of the same elements as part of their statement —access, education for transfer, careers, lifelong learning, contributions to society in a multi-cultural environment — what the statement says, how it is developed and how it is carried out will vary considerably.

Creating or reviewing that mission periodically is an opportunity for Image Team involvement. At some institutions, charrettes are held, bringing together representatives of the internal constituency as well as community representatives, to talk through the meaning and wording of the mission statements and perhaps to further define key directions and goals for the college. Such an activity is probably best done with a facilitator who can listen, interpret and help build consensus.

The Marketing Team

Marketing—defined in its simplest form as finding a need and filling it—is something done in each of our institutions. Done most effectively and viewed in its broadest approach, marketing by definition will cut across lines and involve individuals from a number of areas. How community colleges organize their marketing approaches will create the framework in which all the elements and individuals necessary to market can interact and create an attitude and culture in which to thrive. Marketing can generate one of the largest and most significant image teams.

Marketing is an inclusive process that involves market research; the product itself (curriculum and services), which includes what we offer, and when, where and how we offer it; marketing communications or promotion (often perceived as the only part of marketing); sales or personal contact; and evaluation.

If marketing is indeed "everybody's business," how then does a college take this definition and strategy and put it into action in a complex, busy institution? Consider the following components in a successful college-wide marketing team approach at Cuyahoga Community College.

Gain support and understanding from the top. The college president and trustees set the tone for college marketing campaigns. When Tri-C was interested in initiating a new marketing model, the strategy was first presented to the president and then to the board.

With their understanding of the approach, they were able to endorse the direction and later support resolutions for research and advertising funding. Then, on a regular basis, through the Board's Community Affairs committee, marketing was an ongoing strategic agenda item, and reports were made on progress, accomplishments and directions to keep the board informed and involved.

Develop an organizational framework for marketing. It is impera-

tive that marketing becomes an ongoing, systematic college operation, cutting across division lines and integrated into the college
organization and processes. The president must pro-actively
communicate the relevance of marketing and its function within
college operations.

Secure grassroots involvement. To the greatest extent possible,
everyone at the college must buy into marketing concepts and be
able to offer input for their improvement and use. How might a
college get this grassroots involvement? Here are some possible
strategies:

- Involve as wide a constituency as feasible. Be ready to accept
  and act on input if feasible. Explain when input cannot be
  used.
- Establish a marketing model that defines marketing as
  everyone's responsibility and to everyone's advantage.
- Involve individuals from the earliest planning stages.
- Involve all areas that will implement the plan.
- Once goals and activities are agreed to, empower individuals to
  implement them.
- Create spirit and give recognition to team participants.

Turning to the Voters

Perhaps one of the most inclusive examples of creating image
teams comes through the development of a campaign to pass a tax
levy. While all colleges do not need to do this, the elements
involved clarify and demonstrate a number of important principles
in effective image making and team building.

When trustees place a tax levy on the ballot for voter approval,
they are providing the ultimate test of their community college's
image.   They are asking voters not only to indicate approval for
what the college does, but to demonstrate that approval by paying
for expanded operations. How well the college succeeds in effectively communicating the importance of its role is clearly documented in the outcome of the vote; the feedback is very obvious.
Because a levy is such an open, massive undertaking, it offers a
unique opportunity for the college to communicate its message as

extensively as it ever will. In doing so, however, it exposes the college to exhaustive scrutiny and college leaders need to be ready to answer questions regarding fiscal responsibility, cost effectiveness, and efficient resource utilization. The college will be challenged to defend what it has accomplished as an institution, how it is serving the community, and its expected return on the added investment by the community through the tax levy.

To make the critical decisions for such a campaign, extensive market and opinion research is necessary. Surveys need to tell the institution what level of voter support exists, differences in support among target groups, if any, what services of the institution voters consider most important, what they know and care about its accomplishments. Similar surveys can help keep an institution aware of its image and on target even when a levy is not on the ballot.

With this initial information and analysis in hand, the first hard decisions need to be made by the board, president and top institutional leadership. Is the support there? What level of renewal or increase is really needed and will be supported? What marketing messages are most important? Has everything necessary been done to insure that the college is truly prepared for the intense public scrutiny?

Once the financial analysis and decision to move forward are determined, the key job of identifying clear, simple, compelling messages to be used by the total image team become vital. Under the leadership of the public relations professionals, research results on the institution's benefits that people care about, successes of the institution, and its important roles need to be crafted into a few key points that will be the centerpiece of the image campaign. These key points become the shared message that is carried through campaign leadership, hundreds of volunteers, printed materials, speakers bureau and campaign events.

Who makes up the various image teams in these types of efforts? The key leadership starts, as always, with the board, president, public relations staff and any other appointed executive leadership for such a campaign.

In a recent tax levy campaign at Tri-C, an image team including the president, board chair and other board members, communications professionals and the college treasurer developed a presentation on the financial need and role of the college and met with such groups as leadership from the Chamber of Commerce and County Commissioners. A packet of information that detailed the financial situation included a fact sheet on the college and its students, as well as information on the significant role of the college.

Similar background packets with simpler fact sheets and eventually press releases and printed flyers were developed for all those volunteers who would work with the campaign. Two-minute and ten-minute speeches were developed and disseminated to our speakers bureau, again so we would all be delivering a shared, clear message to the voters.

The leadership team and image team continued to meet with key community outlets for information dissemination and endorsement support, including such groups as the Citizens League, and every major newspaper, television and radio top executive team in the area.

To be successful in passing the levy, however, the image team had to be much broader. Who should be included and how? One key group is often a Citizens Committee to both raise funds and organize a campaign, since by law college operating funds usually cannot be used for the campaign. In looking for this team, recognized community leaders representing the diversity of the community, from politics, business, labor, civic groups, education, ethnic and religious constituencies should be sought to provide leadership to the campaign.

Hopefully, the college will already have established good relations and good image awareness with many of these leaders over the years, so their support is strong at this critical time. Clearly, a levy is passed every day of the year, over the years, and not just during a short campaign blitz.

With this broadened leadership in place at Tri-C, a grassroots campaign structure continued to widen the image team. Literally hundreds of volunteers were needed to carry off the levy campaign. Volunteers were designated by the public relations/marketing staff to handle areas of the county for canvassing, signs, poll coverage, speakers bureau, fund raising, phoning and other aspects.

Students and alumni also became a strong part of the Tri-C image team. A voter registration campaign on campuses was a key element. Students also helped organize a student walk and rally that became major media events. Student leaders were included in college press conferences, and three successful alumni were featured in a series of public service announcements developed for television, showcasing their successes and contributions to the community. Campaign research had revealed that the closer connection individuals had with the college, the more likely they were to support it. Thus, Tri-C students, alumni and employees were its strongest supporters. It further revealed that those who knew the college from visits through activities were also strong supporters, which encouraged Tri-C to expand its on-going community relations and marketing activities well beyond the successful tax levy election.

Expanding the Image Team to Include Community Leaders

Keeping in touch with community leaders is essential if a college is to keep them informed and gain their support. A continuing program of community relations is necessary if colleges expect to have broad-based support and a wide network within the image team. How can colleges develop these types of pro-active relations with community leaders?

A number of approaches can be very successful. One is to develop and continually update a comprehensive college mailing list and make certain that community leaders and organizations from business, politics, education, civic groups, labor, alumni, donors, and prospective donors receive copies of college newsletters, annual reports and announcements of key campus events.

Some type of magazine, newsletter, or annual report should be developed to regularly communicate the college's accomplishments, plans, and directions to the community leadership and other supporters.

Beyond the written word, however, personal contact is also

necessary to achieve the most effective image team building and broaden support with various constituency groups.

Advisory committees. Since community colleges have dozens of career areas, advisory committees to these career programs (required in many states and by some accrediting agencies) offer an excellent avenue for involving individuals in the community college. These advisory committees, composed of top professionals in the respective career fields, serve specifically to help the individual program areas develop appropriate curriculum and remain current and relevant to the needs of the field and community. But as interested individuals, these committee members should be kept more broadly informed about what is happening college-wide. Their input should be sought, and they should be viewed as touchstones for community opinion on the college. Annual appreciation breakfasts or dinners offer an opportunity to recognize advisory committee members for their contributions and to give presentations on the college's goals and progress. These valuable resource persons should also be invited to all major college events.

Legislative relations. Area legislators are key individuals to providing support for future college directions. Regular briefings with these leaders, either individually or in groups, regarding college needs and challenges should be part of a college government relations program. At least annually a legislative event should be planned on campus. A tour of key areas, comments and simple written documents on key needs and issues, and an opportunity to interact with board members, campus leaders and students are possible components of such a visit.

Legislators might also be given figures of the number of students from their area, showing the impact of educational decisions on their specific voting constituencies. Legislators should also be included and recognized in major college events, such as dedications, groundbreakings and anniversaries, particularly including, but not limited to, those where their support provided funding for programs and buildings.

Other community leaders. Leadership and image teams can also be further identified in the community. Some colleges put together a list of 100 or so opinion leaders and invite them to a special briefing breakfast three or four times a year. For each briefing, one or two particular programs or directions are selected, and presentations made. These can range from the new technology centers to elders programs, fine arts productions to tech prep, or an endless number of college accomplishments. Time for questions and for informal interaction between college and community leaders should also be allowed at these sessions.

The Internal Image Team

It is also important to create internal image teams to carry the college message to the community. This starts with keeping the college employees well informed about issues, challenges, and opportunities. Sometimes colleges focus so much energy on the news media and community groups they forget to start with the most important resource, college employees.

First and foremost, college employees must be kept informed and given opportunities to ask questions and share ideas. Regular written communications and newsletters are a start. Informal employee forums can also be organized periodically as another means to accomplish this.

Employees shouldn't have to learn about important college announcements by reading about them in the local newspaper. Written information should be scheduled to appear on employees' desks at the same time it is being released to newspapers for key announcements. A telephone hotline with an up-to-the-minute message is another means of regular internal communication.

Bringing the Community to the Campus

In addition to community leaders, focus needs to be placed on bringing a broad cross-section of the grassroots community to campus as often as possible so they too become, in effect, image team members. College activities, therefore, can play an important role in image building simply by creating familiarity with the college and good feelings for it through activities that physically bring people, who would otherwise not come, to the campus. Once on campus, individuals tend to be very impressed with the facilities and programs and become more likely to want to learn more about what the college can offer them and others in the community. Positive experiences at college events can easily lead to future support.

Campus events can also serve as a non-threatening way to recruit potential students, particularly non-traditional students. Older students may be hesitant to take that first giant step to return to education, but may be more likely to take the risk once they have some familiarity with the campus after having attended an event there.

What kinds of events can bring the community to the campus? The possibilities are endless:

- Special events, open to the community. As much as possible, keeping these free (or low cost) and open to the public helps attract a broader base of individuals and shows how the college serves the community.

  Typical events can include sports competitions, plays, lectures, and concerts. Unusual campus events can further make your activities compete with the wide range at other community organizations, as well as garner media attention. For example, at Cuyahoga Community College, bringing the traveling model of the Vietnam Wall to campus drew 10,000 from the community. An annual Martin Luther King Jr. program brings overflow crowds annually to hear the Cleveland Philharmonic Orchestra and some other performances in honor of Dr. King and gives a chance to focus on his message of equity and opportunity, both embraced by the community college.

  Large scale community open houses and scholarship benefits provide opportunities not only to bring thousands to the Tri-C campuses for the events themselves, but to build media attention and support for the college as well.

- Use of campus facilities for community groups. Many of the community colleges have outstanding facilities for meetings, sports events, and performances. Allowing the community to use these facilities at times when they are not used for classroom or college purposes endears the college to the comunity and serves to again bring diverse individuals to the campus. Charging reasonable rates that cover expenses can be part of this relationship.

Special Events on a Grand Scale

Anniversaries, groundbreakings, dedications, inaugurations, and graduations provide opportunities to create major events that involve the entire community, attract major media attention, and create image teams to carry out these events.

One community college's anniversary celebrations, for example, used a scholarship benefit dinner-dance as its centerpiece, bringing together the development, alumni and public relations functions. It began with an analysis of the college's goals, which included spreading the message of the success of its students, its quality faculty and education, and its upcoming focus on high technology. To carry out this message, the event, called MegaFest, used a futuristic theme complete with robots and high tech decorations and entertainment. In all, the event attracted 2,000 to the dinner-dance representing a broad cross-section of the community, another 4,000 to other related events, raised $43,000, resulted in hundreds of print and broadcast stories and strengthened the college's alumni association.

What kind of image teams are necessary to carry out such massive undertakings? Planning begins with college leadership and the public relations/marketing units to establish goals and basic directions. To draw community support, a citizens planning team, selected for diversity much as a levy team would be, can help involve the community from the early stages and can bring the community in to the event once it is planned. Internally, image teams are also established, turning to those whose expertise is critical to the event, such as artists, security, cultural arts, audio-visual, and maintenance staff, so that, like marketing teams, input is sought in the beginning, and enthusiasm is built across organizational lines.

For the inauguration of its new president, Tri-C again used the occasion to focus on the role of the college in serving its students. As part of this, a special benefit luncheon raised $89,000 in scholarship funds. An external committee, chaired by two well-known community leaders and event planners, and guided by internal image teams, approached area companies and organizations to sponsor tables. The inauguration ceremony itself gave an opportunity for various community leaders to interact with the college and hear the message of its role in serving the area.

These event examples show how valuable an interrelation between internal image teams and broader external constituencies can be. The overall positive image created and communicated through public relations activities solidifies the college image and shares messages that carry forward and build on community support for future college initiatives.

For community colleges, and particularly those that depend on local tax revenues for major support, the broad community is always a target audience. Some activities, however, are designed to serve a more specific targeted segment of the community and events and activities can be designed to develop those image teams.

Partnerships to Serve the Community

Economic development partnerships are a good example of this type of special relationship. Perhaps one of the most significant roles of community colleges today is their contribution to workforce development that will help keep American businesses competitive in the local and global marketplace.

A technology center, offering customized training to business and industry, can establish partnerships with government agencies and private business and industry. Such joint ventures bind business leaders to the college through their perceptions of its image and its ability to meet their needs; once involved, they share their expertise and ultimately become yet another image team to carry a message of what the community college can do.

Partnerships with other educational institutions also serve the community college well and expand the team of those who under-stand it. Dual enrollments with four-year universities help commu-

nity college students transfer and send a message of quality.
Similarly, relationships with secondary school systems, through
advanced placement, motivational programs, tech prep and other
partnerships help high school students consider continuing education and help the community see inter-relationships and resource
sharing in education.

Coalitions Beyond the Community

The work done by the community college and its ability to communicate that work to its various constituencies serve as the basis for
the college's image. However, the quality and value of all community colleges, higher education, and, in fact, education in general, on
a local, regional, and national basis has an impact on a specific
college as well. Paying attention to these commentaries, as well as
forming coalitions beyond our own colleges, is another way to create
significant image teams.

Given current challenges and opportunities, community
colleges have entered an era when higher education may be as
important as it has ever been. Seventy-five percent of all new jobs
by the year 2000 will require postsecondary education. The
majority of newcomers to the workforce will be women and minorities. Businesses need skilled workers to do the jobs in a age of
changing technology. More than half of all college freshmen are in
community colleges. It is not surprising then, that the effectiveness
of community colleges is under scrutiny, simply because the need
for them to be effective is so critical.

Thus, issues such as transfer rates and success rates become
questions raised nationally about community colleges. And issues
of faculty teaching vs. research, tenure, and escalating tuition costs
become questions for all of higher education. Community college
leaders must be aware of these issues since they are the context for
our local community colleges. And they must be prepared to
provide the public with answers, using their own colleges as
examples, if they are to create images that truly reflect the work
being done. Trustees need to be able to cite the transfer rates of
their students, the job placement rates of career programs, the

success of their students who transfer, and the fiscal efficiencies of their institution. In light of the national scrutiny, community college leaders need to have answers to these questions and then communicate them.

Coalitions among colleges are one way to provide information to the public and to legislatures who fund our operations. Joining together with other colleges, whether in an expanded greater city, state or national coalition gives colleges a number of advantages:

- Each has the benefit of added thinking and resources—personnel as well as financial
- Communications made jointly are stronger, receive more attention, and show that issues are neither parochial nor tied up in the agenda of just one college.
- A coalition shows colleges working together and perhaps even pooling resources, almost mandatory in today's hard economic times.

And so, colleges in a number of states have joined together to create information and image campaigns to pass important legislation, to focus on the value of community colleges through media campaigns. These state organizations vary in composition, some made up of presidents, some of trustees. In many, the group has a separate council of the communications professionals who work with presidents and trustees to plan and implement image and information campaigns.

In Greater Cleveland, for example, the Cleveland Commission on Higher Education organized an image campaign for its 17 member colleges around the theme of Campus One, showing the diversity of college opportunities in Greater Cleveland and organizing an 800 number and computer followup system for inquiries of students interested in college information. Both two- and four-year colleges joined to focus on the importance of education, the rich resources available locally, as well as the economic impact of these colleges collectively.

In Texas, a statewide coalition, the Texas Public Community/

Junior College Association, composed of presidents, has a communications council responsible for a number of successful image, news and legislative campaigns. They planned a statewide billboard campaign for Community College Month featuring community college graduate Nolan Ryan, organized an exhibit in the State Capitol rotunda for state legislators, and had a day at the State Fair declared Community College Day.

National Community College Month, co-sponsored in April by the American Association of Community Colleges, the National Council for Marketing and Public Relations, and the Association of Community College Trustees, is, in fact, an excellent opportunity to create a national focus that can serve as a springboard for communicating the significant role of your community college. A full promotion kit is available to colleges through NCMPR, ACCT or AACC, and includes such resources as press releases, advertisements, proclamations and special events that can be used during this month. It gives all community colleges, whether individually or in college coalitions, an opportunity to build on their regular ongoing techniques of media and community relations to tell the community college story.

Telling the Story through the Media

How can the community college story be told effectively through the media on an on-going basis? While the responsibility is primarily led by the public relations professional, here again, an image team that cooperates successfully expands the possibilities for good media relations.

On an on-going basis, visits to the editorial boards and top leadership of the area's key newspapers, radio and television outlets should be made by the president, public relations professional and perhaps the board chair. These meetings should create relationships of trust, understanding of the broad picture of the college and its key concerns, directions, and accomplishments. This basis of understanding will serve the institution well and help keep issues in perspective when individual stories or questions surface.

Through memos from public relations and personal follow-up,

faculty, administrators, and trustees can also be encouraged to write opinion pieces for editorial pages, or add their names to a list of experts made available to the media spokespersons on a variety of topics. All these highlight the quality of community college faculty and positively reflect the overall image of a college.

But what about those times when the college faces issues that are sensitive or controversial? Who is responsible then, and how do college's deal with the news media in these image-threatening situations. Crises today can range from the life threatening situations of hurricanes, dangerous accidents and crime, to strikes, lawsuits, and questions about the institution's effectiveness. How well college leaders respond or react — taking an honest, proactive, non-defensive, problem-solving approach—is as important as the crisis situation itself.

As in other image situations, a clearly planned, written approach that delineates responsibilities will help an institution meet these challenges effectively. The time to prepare for a crisis is not when one strikes, but in advance by anticipating how the college will act and react.

Determining a spokesperson will be one of the key factors in dealing with media in sensitive situations, as well as knowing who makes the decisions, how to communicate with key leaders within and outside the institution, and deciding who has to be informed and by whom. Certainly this communications loop, like so many others, must include at least the president, board chair and chief public relations professional.

Generally, the chief PR professional is the designated spokesperson, but it may be best for others to respond depending on the situation—the president, perhaps the board chair or an expert on the question at hand, whether it's the athletic director or nursing dean. Others in an institution may be contacted by the media, and in fact may want to and will speak in controversial situations, but the designated spokesperson gives the official college position. What is to be said as the official college statement should be discussed by the PR professional, president, board chair, or others, and preferably put in writing so that all stakeholders have the same information and a common message is clear to all involved in responding. Possible questions should be anticipated and reviewed. The spokesperson must then provide information accurately, quickly and consistently.

Those who may be called should be informed. Trustees, for example, may be called by the newspaper regardless who the college has decided is the spokesperson. They should know, as should others in the institution, that they personally may or may not wish to respond or to respond immediately, although the college must respond. It is acceptable, if not preferable, to have the board chairman speak for the board. Board members can also refer a reporter to the college-determined spokesperson.

Many factors in responding to a crisis should be part of the plan created in advance and discussed and disseminated among college leadership. Briefings, workshops on media relations for college leadership, and anticipation of potential issues will serve the institution well.

Perhaps the best way a college can ride through a crisis is to have public opinion/media already on the side of the college because it has been doing good, positive communication all along, through image teams and other efforts. A wide community constituency that understands and supports the institution will help the college survive any crisis situation.

Keeping the Image Team in Place

The image teams that community colleges create and nurture must become a part of the college culture. "Community" is the word that defines community colleges. To truly serve the community, college leaders must involve the community. This chapter has reviewed a number of ways to define, reach and involve a variety of image teams. The more this involvement takes place, the more able college leaders are to assess community needs and develop community trust and support. And the more community support that colleges have, the better they can do their jobs.

Celebrating a Province-Wide Anniversary

Ontario colleges had a unique opportunity in 1992 to make public their mission and merits. Most Ontario colleges were established in 1967; consequently, 1992 was designated as the system's 25th anniversary year.

A provincial committee was established, chaired by Richard Johnston, head of the Council of Regents for Ontario's 23 colleges. Membership on the committee came from several sources, including alumni, public affairs personnel, college governors and presidents, students, athletics and recreational personnel, the Ministry of Colleges and Universities, the Ontario Public Service Employees Union, and the Association of Colleges of Applied Arts and Technology of Ontario (ACAATO).

The group developed, discussed and decided upon a number of activities to be sponsored province-wide. One activity was a proposal from the College Advisory Committee on Public Affairs (CACPA), the association of communications and public relations professionals from Ontario's colleges. The project involved working with *The Globe and Mail*, a Toronto-based national newspaper, to produce a special supplement highlighting how colleges contribute to their communities and the economy.

The Globe and Mail was chosen not only because of its scope and reputation, but also because its readership profile is an older, more affluent, executive one — leaders in business, industry and government.

In consultation with the newspaper's representatives, members of CACPA devised, developed and assisted *Globe and Mail* staff with articles and visuals related to selected themes: unique programs, centers of excellence, innovative partnerships, links with business and industry, special needs and minority group initiatives, international activities, access programs, environmental projects and community outreach.

Advertising, arranged through CACPA, ACAATO and the College Committee on Resource Development (CCRD) primarily featured partnership messages — each advertisement pairing one college with one of its primary corporate supporters.

The result? On September 11, 1992, *The Globe and Mail*'s Ontario and Quebec editions (272,000 copies) contained *A Sense of Community*, a ten-page supplement which succeeded in making a strong, positive statement about the unique value of colleges in Ontario.

by John Sawicki, Manager, Communications
Conestoga College
Kitchener, Ontario, Canada

Marketing: A Model Plan

Lane Community College in Eugene, Oregon, is a large school: nearly 1,000 employees serving more than 33,000 students a year. We have a successful marketing program. Yet when we calculate the size of our public relations staff for the Paragon Award competition, at 2.85 professionals, we barely make it into the "B", or large school, category.

So we asked ourselves, how are we able to run such a diverse program for a large institution with a relatively small staff? The answer lies in our model for organizing and funding marketing.

Lane has a college-wide marketing council with 27 members representing all branches of the college and composed of faculty, staff and students. The council has nine subcommittees, whose chairs serve as a steering committee for the council. The council is chaired by the Director of Institutional Advancement, who oversees development of the marketing plan and administers a centralized institutional marketing budget; however, the work is spread throughout the college and the nine subcommittees.

To illustrate, one subcommittee focuses on improving services and information to returning women students. This subcommittee is chaired by the coordinator of the college's Women's Center and each year hosts a "Women's Day on Campus" which attracts 300-400 women. The marketing council provides ideas and feedback, the centralized marketing budget pays for the event, and the women's subcommittee of the council and Women's Center staff carry it out. This division of labor is repeated through the work of each of the nine subcommittees.

Another link the Institutional Advancement office and marketing council have with the campus community is through a program of grants to departments that wish to undertake their own marketing activities. Departments submit a written application. If the project is approved, the centralized marketing budget provides the funding, Institutional Advancement staff provide technical advice, and the department implements the project itself.

Over the years, Marketing Council grants have funded several dozen applications and helped to launch a number of interesting activities, for example, providing the seed money for a poster created by second year graphic design students to promote the graphic design program. The four-color poster displayed the newly designed business cards of the graduating graphics design students, becoming a part of each student's portfolio as well as a valuable recruitment tool for the department.

This approach to marketing works well for Lane. The close involvement of both the Institutional Advancement office and the Marketing Council ensures consistency and coordination across campus and provides a mechanism for quality control, while the implementation of activities is done by staff in individual college departments who know their clients and programs better than Advancement staff do. The result are activities that are on target and generally effective.

There are other advantages as well. The college's marketing plan is reviewed and refined each year by the council and subcommittees. Because the funding is maintained in a centralized budget, rather than divided up and housed in several dozen individual department budgets, money can be shifted to meet the most important priority. This keeps the overall budget in check and encourages us to eliminate lower priority activities.

There also has been an unanticipated benefit to this approach. This model has been in place at Lane since 1985 and predated the current community college emphasis on working in cross-campus teams, shared decision making, and continuous quality improvement. Yet it encapsulates many of these principles and has been cited on- and off-campus as a model of participation. With colleges across the country struggling to integrate these concepts, this praise and recognition, albeit less tangible, means as much to us as our Paragon Awards.

by Diane DuVal Dann
Associate Director of Institutional Advancement
Lane Community College
Eugene, Oregon

CHAPTER 5

Special Challenges

by Larry Bracken
Director, College Advancement
Pensacola Junior College

and Karen Jones
Assistant to the President
for Communications and Alumni
Lower Columbia College

About the Authors

Larry Bracken and Karen Jones

Larry Bracken is District Director for College Advancement at Pensacola Junior College (Florida), a position he has held since 1983. Prior to that he was Director of Public Relations for Garland County Community College in Hot Springs, Arkansas. Bracken has experience in public relations, marketing, media relations, and government relations. He lives in Gulf Breeze, Florida, and lectures and consults in higher education media relations and marketing.

Karen Jones has been with the Communications Office at Lower Columbia College in Longview, Washington, since 1982. She serves as Assistant to the President for Communications and Alumni Relations and is responsible for college relations and communications, special events, legislative contact and alumni activities. An active member of the Washington Community College Public Information Commission, Karen is past president of the National Council for Marketing and Public Relations.

Let's pretend we have a hypothetical community college which is doing everything right: faculty, administration and classified staff are competent and enlightened; instructional programs are comprehensive and technologically timely; marketing and image- building activities are efficient and effective; internal and external communications are thorough and honest; students are successful, morale is high and millages pass with high percentages at wonderful Camelot Community College. It's not unreasonable to expect all the above could come together in one place, on one campus...occasionally...for a few brief, shining moments.

During their history, two-year community, junior and technical colleges have survived prosperous and lean years, have experienced shake-ups and shake-downs, and have used their responsive natures to meet challenges dictated by exigencies, natural and otherwise. However, even the most accountable, creative and successful institutions, like our mythical Camelot Community College, cannot avoid today's curses. Let's take a look at some of the intense pressures on higher education today and the impacts they can have on a college's image.

Living (and Surviving) with the Media

The phenomenal increase of American community colleges coincided, in the 1960s and 1970s, with a new age of American journalism. This new media arrived with a philosophy of post-Watergate adversarial journalism and was armed with a new technology of mini-cams, recorders, and freedom of information laws. Community colleges, often born in deserted shopping centers or abandoned high schools, were, and still are, essentially populist institutions, seeking to serve a broad constituency of the public and dedicated to community service. Community colleges were new, innovative, and anxious to cure the higher education ills of any community.

It was a shock when the media began, in the 1980s, to bring two-year institutions under their growing umbrella of scrutiny. The media suddenly appeared to be embarked on a policy of attacking, even ambushing, community colleges. Just as suddenly, community college trustees and administrators became concerned about their public image and with their equally important legislative image.

It was obvious from the beginning that the best way for new community colleges to reach the public, to provide information about courses, registration, and programs, was through the local newspapers, radio and television stations. New, as well as established institutions were welcomed by communities and, in general, the local media provided a supportive voice for these new local community colleges. Older, more developed "junior colleges" expanded curricula to include comprehensive credit and non-credit offerings, cultural events, open libraries, athletic programs, student services and the host of other activities that make up today's community colleges. These changes were supported by editorial boards, reporters, television news teams, and publishers.

The often perplexing adversarial media scrutiny of community colleges began during the late 1970s and 1980s, as news organizations began to place other aspects of society under a media microscope. Newspapers that had carried editorials of praise for the community college missions, began to demand public documents. Articles based on statements by disgruntled employees appeared, along with requests for salary and benefit details. Radio and television stations, once glad to give free air time, now had reporters on campus, videotape rolling, demanding full disclosure of board of trustee policies, and explanations of the value of programs and activities. Presidents, recently praised by the media, found themselves confronting difficult questions and accusations about institutional operations. Board of trustee members found themselves defending a growing variety of college initiatives, procedures, practices and policies.

In essence, the shining image of community colleges began to show tarnish. Board members, presidents, and deans began to question the perceived supportive role of the media. In the minds of community college professionals, the cherished "positive" image seemed to be on the verge of replacement by a "negative" image. This fear was fostered by a skeptical media and a public growing suspicious of public institutions in general.

In actuality, this change represented a "coming of age" for American community colleges. From a media perspective, local community colleges had survived infancy, and had matured to the level of legitimate public institutions, much as universities, city councils, county commissions, health care agencies, and public schools. Community colleges were no longer unique or deserving of special treatment. Maturity as by recognized community entities brought the responsibilities that governmental units eventually all must face: financial scrutiny and accountability; full-blown public relations and marketing plans; a demand for governmental oversight; and competitive programs and intensified auditing procedures.

Today's community college trustees and administrators are faced with the necessity to work with media—local, regional and national. This relationship reflects current public opinion that higher education has unique strengths and weaknesses. The "image" of higher education is diverse, ranging from traditional American faith and trust in the value of postsecondary education to concerns about the growing costs and tax burden of our educational system. National higher education issues are "localized" by newspapers, radio and television. Wire service reports of national average tuition increases become local stories. Student loan default stories from Washington, D.C., result in reporter inquiries to local community colleges regarding loan default rates. Sexual harassment policies, AIDS on campus issues, athletic expenditures, collective bargaining issues, insurance liability concerns and lawsuits, all become legitimate topics for the news media. Add to this list the media concerns of salaries, travel expenditures, and other emerging concerns, such as minority graduation rates, costly athletic programs, and gay and lesbian student policies.

Because the coverage of community colleges had historically been positive, trustees and administrators began to view any adversarial questioning by the media as a "crisis." In fact, few media issues are really "crises." In a mature institutional setting such concerns should be viewed in broader categorical terms: issues, emergencies, and crises.

Trustees and administrators should attempt to maintain broad involvement in national, state and local higher education issues. Involvement in organizations such as the Association of Community College Trustees (ACCT) and the American Association of Community Colleges (AACC) can help keep agendas up-dated. Readership of the national press helps maintain focus. A review of such publications as the *Community College Times*, various ACCT reports and newsletters and the *Chronicle of Higher Education* can assist in identifying evolving issues. Stories on higher education issues in the *New York Times*, *Wall Street Journal*, CNN, or even the plethora of news/informational television, from "60 Minutes" to "Oprah," can also identify issues.

Information needs to be disseminated in a professional manner and contingency responses prepared, either formally or informally. No trustee or administrator can keep pace with the increasing flux of information. Every institution has key personnel in public information and public relations offices that can monitor issues. Some college information offices utilize "issue papers" to keep trustees and administrators informed of issues that might attract the attention of the local media. Anticipation and knowledge of emerging issues is the only manner of preparing for intelligent responses to media issue concerns. Issues range from homeless students to the availability of condoms on campus. Issues include concerns regarding AIDS, budget cuts, personnel layoffs, and graduation rates, among others.

Issues that attract media attention are often opportunities to inform and educate the public, a legitimate and necessary role of community colleges. Few local colleges can exist in such isolation as to avoid broader higher education issues, nor should they. The media provides a means of informing the public about these important issues. It is a mistake to view the media as simply disrespectful detractors of an institution's public image.

Emergencies sometimes impact institutions and require professional responses. The exact nature of emergencies is difficult

to predict, but many can be anticipated. Many colleges have plans
for snowstorms or hurricanes, but true emergencies, which attract
media attention, are often surprises.

For instance, it is one of the ironies of higher education that
everyone is invited onto our campuses. Community colleges strive
to serve a broad and diverse segment of the public and, consequently, populations of community colleges are reflections of our
society. All types of individuals make up collective student bodies.

Theft, assault, violence, and other aspects of society are as
much a part of campus life as of any community. Response to these
issues involve law enforcement reaction that includes campus
security, as well as city, county, and state agencies. Emergencies
which originate outside institutional purview— criminal acts or
natural disasters such as fire, hurricanes or tornadoes— can devas-
tate a college community.

In these cases media coverage may impact an institution's
image. These situations, however, are usually taken over and
controlled by law enforcement or fire fighting professionals, or by
civil defense or disaster agencies. While it is important to provide
concise and accurate information during such emergencies, most
information released to the media is filtered through the agency
conducting the investigation or responding to the situation.

The impact of such emergencies on the image of the institution
is usually minimal. The public appears to understand that the
institution is not responsible for unanticipated violence, catastro-
phe, or natural disaster. If a college has taken normal and reasonable steps to maintain order and safety, and has adequately communicated its actions internally and externally, the public is usually
sympathetic to the institutional problems.

*Perhaps the most important concern is to make sure that routine
emergency procedures and policies are developed and that appropriate
responses are planned and carried out.* Any institution judged by the
public, through the filter of the media, to be negligent or not
prepared, will suffer a negative impact.

The media does have a legitimate interest in issues related to
the operations, both internal and external, of public institutions.
The First Amendment to the Constitution of the United States is

one of the foundations of American democracy, but it is an easy
concept to forget when one is being queried by a local newspaper
reporter. The importance of freedom of information statutes may be
difficult to keep in focus if a television video camera is rolling while
a reporter is pressing for details about administrative salaries. The
last thing on the mind of a trustee is the intrinsic legal value of
freedom of information (state sunshine) laws while carrying on a
late-night telephone conversation with a reporter concerning a
lawsuit filed by a former employee.

*Personnel at all levels of institutions of higher education should
understand, appreciate, and jealously guard the constitutional rights of the
media.* Not only does the media serve as the conduit for much of
any college's information, public relations and marketing program,
but the media also provides the public with information regarding
the governmental function of the institution. A mature institution
must operate with a professional respect for the value of the media
to educate, inform, and enlighten the same public that the colleges
seek to serve. It is perhaps ironic that media bashing can take place
on the same campuses that teach journalism, history, and political
science.

There are legitimate and professional means for working with
the media to insure that rights and responsibilities of both the
media and colleges are protected. Internal procedures should be in
place to make sure that institutional representatives can respond to
the media in a clear, concise, accurate and timely fashion. Trustees
and administrators should work closely with the college's public
relations or public information office to determine how best to work
with the media. Working together does not mean that diverse
opinions on subjects of interest are to be discouraged. But working
together to present a common set of concerns to the media is
important.

Campus Crime and Security Issues

Community colleges, concerned about their images as open door
institutions, face a growing array of crime and security problems
that impact public opinion and institutional image. Because most

admission policies of community colleges read like the inscription on the Statue of Liberty, these new issues are encroaching on already limited resources.

Community colleges invite everyone onto campus, regardless of their academic records, police records, or psychological profiles. We pride ourselves on the fact that we will take a risk on any person. Because institutions are microcosms of society, they will have some individuals on campus who they might not truly want. In addition, there is a mystique that college and university campuses are secure and safe sanctuaries. The series of students murdered at the University of Florida and Santa Fe Community College have dispelled that myth.

Rising reports of campus crime, ranging from assault and rape to theft and concealed weapons, worry trustees and administrators. This has resulted in increased campus security costs, and legislation requiring open reports on campus crime. This has often presented an unusual negative image to the public. What kind of colleges do we have when there are muggings in our parking lots? In truth, no college or university or public place of any kind is immune to crime.

New discussions are beginning in which colleges are debating spending shrinking dollars on increasing campus security forces. In addition, a new consideration is whether or not to arm campus security officers. To many of today's college administrators— and trustees— raised in the '60s— armed campus security officers recall images of campus riots and clashes of the Vietnam War era. Images of Kent State, of police lines around administration buildings, and office takeovers come uneasily to mind.

However, community colleges today face a far different need for campus security. More than half of our students are women, many older women. Most are alert, savvy, and security conscious. They share the same concerns about community college parking lots as they do about shopping mall parking lots. They demand well-lighted facilities and evident campus security. And most community colleges must provide it or face possible legal liability and negative publicity.

Since most campuses are open, a new problem facing some

colleges, especially urban locations, is that of the homeless on campus. This same problem faces local governments, where homeless individuals and groups have taken refuge in public parks, restrooms, and other public facilities. Colleges are looking for solutions to the problem, but their universal invitation impedes the ability to regulate and control college facilities.

As colleges have stocked their classrooms and labs with expensive computer equipment, costly audio-visual equipment, including color televisions and VCRs, the problem of felony theft has grown. Lightweight computers, printers, and CD ROM equipment is costly and easily removed. The cost of property control and of securing equipment has risen dramatically.

Classrooms and labs have always been left open to a large degree, but today doors must be locked, and detection systems installed. College insurance policies require no less vigilance and limited budgets cannot afford to be eroded by replacement costs in addition to constant upgrading costs. Yet such attempts to provide safety and security, to deal with indigent individuals, and the armed camp mentality do not play well in the area of public opinion and certainly produce a negative impact on a community college's image.

Increased Governmental Regulation and Oversight

The last ten years have seen a formidable increase in state and federal accountability mandates, regulations, and documentation requirements for business in general and public agencies in particular. With these raised expectations of desired results by everyone from governmental agencies to environmental groups come increased areas of exposure for community colleges.

Compliance with measures such as the Americans with Disabilities Act, affirmative action plans, the Safe Campus Act, and student and employee right-to-know laws places increased pressure on college staff and financial resources. At some colleges additional employees have been hired solely to carry out reporting requirements. They are the fortunate institutions. At most colleges these duties have been spread among already burdened existing staff.

Add to these increased duties the additional costs of services and retrofiting facilities, and the compliance monkey has suddenly taken on the proportions of King Kong.

When we can set the monster down for a minute and take a look at it, three things become apparent:

- Colleges cannot escape compliance and bureaucratic red tape;
- All these requirements, in one way or another, address better service to our students or prospective students;
- With the commitment and participation of each college constituent group, we can not only meet our obligations, but turn these new charges into advantages.

Traditionally, community and technical colleges have served those who, through the lack of finances, mobility or prior education, don't have the choices of others seeking higher education. These regulations directly address the needs of students and require us to equalize the ways that colleges deliver opportunity.

It is therefore incumbent upon trustees and administrators to have a full understanding and appreciation of the requirements and the heart of these acts, laws and rules. That education must be communicated to faculty, staff and student workers. They are not only employees spending a better part of their waking hours at our colleges; they are also our front-line representatives to the public.

Moreover, the messages we must include and services we must provide give us an opportunity to present all the personal positives that make two-year colleges unique. Although it is arguable that any student would stop using drugs because we give them a brochure on their ill effects once a year, the recurring statement of the unacceptability of drug use sets a standard that speaks to who we are. Published photos recognizing the diversity of our student populations reveal our effectiveness at reaching across cultural barriers.

Carpe brochurum, as they say in public information offices.

Escalating Litigation

When the NCMPR Board was determining what, if any, insurance it should be carrying, the members asked their attorney where they might be exposed to suits or claims. "Today," said the attorney, "anybody can sue anyone for anything." This kind of public exposure is true for public agencies not only in the realm of lawsuits, but also in areas such as compensation claims and oversight from other agencies. It is not uncommon to have one state agency bring a suit against another—a case of the right hand demanding blood from the left elbow.

Colleges are also increasingly caught in the conflict of an individual's right to privacy and public disclosure. If college leaders don't know the answers to these important legal questions, they must discover:

What files in offices are subject to search and seizure by the press under public disclosure laws?

Are files kept at a faculty member's home still considered public record?

Is anything private in the college's Public Information Office?

What should not be kept in files?

How much information can a college release on students? On employees?

What is considered "confidential" and what isn't?

The answers to these questions are critical for both "success story" articles (low pressure) or media crises (high pressure). Answers will also vary from state to state. But college leaders must be acutely aware of these issues because there is an increased sensitivity to real and imagined slights and negligence and there is a growing population willing to find out what benefits the legal system can yield.

Wise college leaders have sound legal counsel, faith in that counsel, and a solid structure for communicating necessary information regarding the above questions to its employees. Campus leadership must have an appreciation of its own and the outside world's legal prerogatives and ensure that its campus community is sensitized to issues of privacy and public disclosure. These are all ideal topics for inservice training seminars.

Capitol Report: Legislative Issues

Since the major portion of funding for higher education comes from state legislatures, community college trustees and administrators must constantly work to maintain a positive image with elected state representatives. In times of tight budgets, budget shortfalls, calls for "right sizing," "down sizing," and "retrenchment", the relationship with elected representatives takes on increased importance. The flow of appropriation dollars to institutions is not totally dependent upon the image of respective institutions, but it is an important factor. Problems, difficulties, audit criticisms, employee unrest, declining enrollments, and other issues, funneled through the media to state capitols, can have a negative impact on operational budgets. Additionally, new issues are constantly appearing on the legislative horizon.

In some states new public concerns such as growth management are beginning to impact public image. Where does the responsibility begin and end for such diverse community issues as traffic flow, run-off of water from paved parking lots, and the use of the land itself? If our institutions grow, causing increased traffic, who will pay for the widening of roads, for the costly traffic signals, and for the increased demand on water and sewer systems? Hard pressed local and state governments are beginning to consider the possibility of passing those costs on to colleges.

In an era of increasing sensitivity to the environment, such growth management issues and infrastructure demands may cause damage to institutional image. Such basic philosophical questions as "is growth really progress?" may have to be answered by community, technical and junior colleges.

Can appropriations keep pace with growth needs? Even with the multiplicity of funding models spread across the country and increased support from foundations and grants, community colleges cannot keep up with enrollment pressures caused by a growing population, skyrocketing tuition in four-year colleges and a workforce in continual need of retraining.

However, when faced with recessionary times, with the demands on state budgets for health care needs, elder care, transportation, law enforcement, and corrections, there are always many other needs that require fiscal support. In such times, legislators may not respond well to the increased needs of public education and university systems.

One answer increasingly heard in state capitols is the need to limit the growth of higher education institutions, including the community colleges. A cornerstone of the positive philosophical image of community colleges has been the "open door" concept. Can states afford to continue to fund the growth of community colleges? Will the "open door" gradually close and enrollment limits be placed on institutions dedicated to community education and service? If so, how will our colleges determine who shall be admitted? These are serious issues that trustees and administrators may face in the not too distant future.

Is remedial education the responsibility of community colleges (or universities) or should that expense be passed back to public school districts which initially failed to provide the necessary minimal math and reading skills? Should community colleges be involved in adult education or continuing education?

New accountability standards are being discussed in almost every state legislature. Headcount funding gave way to FTE (full time equivalency) funding years ago. Some legislative leaders are suggesting that graduation rates may be a more reasonable means of funding. Still others suggest that job placement may be a better factor in determining funding levels.

Other issues, including collective bargaining by faculty and career service employees can impact the image of any institution. A growing demand for the use of fewer part-time and adjunct faculty members, accompanied by a need to improve compensation for those important faculty members are both on today's community college legislative agendas.

Other new legislative challenges include attempts to maintain currency with evolving computer and information technology, establish linkages with business and industry, and improve articulation between crowded community colleges and equally crowded universities. Competition between school districts, community colleges and universities for funds and for students continues to escalate. Many of these issues will be debated before state legislatures and new regulations, statues, and regulations will result. Some will be in keeping with the traditional community college image and others will detract from the historical mission of two-year colleges. All will involve institutional image, how colleges are viewed by their communities, their students, their faculty, and by the higher education community.

The Challenges of Maturity

If community colleges are to garner the respect of the public, then an understanding of contemporary issues, and the anticipation of future issues, is an absolute necessity. In the end it is the role of trustees and administrators to make the policy decisions that determine the long-term effectiveness of the institution.

All institutions have trained professionals working in college public relations, public information, media relations, marketing departments, and advancement offices. Their duty is to keep abreast of issues, to prepare institutional responses to issues, to work objectively with the media, to provide accurate information to the media. Trustees and administrators should learn to fully utilize the professionalism and experience of such college staff.

In *Reinventing Government*, David Osborne and Ted Gaebler wrote:

> We live in an era of breathtaking change. We live in a global marketplace, which puts enormous competitive pressure on our economic institutions. We live in an information society, in which people get access to information almost as fast as their leaders do. We live in a knowledge-based economy, in which educated workers bridle at commands and demand autonomy...Today's environment demands institutions that are extremely flexible and adaptable. It demands institutions that deliver high-quality goods and services, squeezing ever more bang out of every buck. It demands institutions that are

responsive to their customers, offering choices of nonstandardized services...It demands institutions that empower citizens rather than simply serving them.

This description of their acclaimed New Paradigm could also be a description of today's mature, responsible community college, providing comprehensive higher educational opportunities to American citizens.

REFERENCE

David Osborne and Ted Gaebler: *Reinventing Government*, Addison-Wesley Publishing Company, Inc. Reading Massachusetts, 1992, page 15.

The Battle Over Art

The front page *Orlando Sentinel* morning headline read: "Explicit art at Valencia draws protest from religious leaders." It was the first article in what became a public debate about what is art and what responsibility a college has to taxpayers who may disagree.

The art exhibit, titled "Scents and Shivers," by Georgia artist Bill Paul, mixed religious symbolism with stark images of suffering to draw an analogy between the persecution of people with AIDS and the persecution of Jesus Christ. It was reported in *USA Today, The Atlanta Constitution*, and the *Miami Herald*, and became a three-month topic on local talk radio. It sparked a national campaign against Valencia Community College by the Christian Coalition.

Valencia responded quickly by gathering relevant information. We talked with the people who selected the exhibit. We toured the show with the curator and art faculty. Our exhibit was grant-funded, so we read the grant proposal carefully. We learned everything relevant about the artist. We made certain that our position would be defensible.

We gathered copies of favorable reviews, including one by the *Orlando Sentinel* art critic who praised the work. We located the college's policy statement on academic freedom and the art gallery's statement of purpose. We also collected any favorable remarks written in the gallery visitors log.

We then offered the college president a well-researched position statement and explained how adopting it would help minimize damage. Copies of the position paper were provided to all the key players, including the trustees. The carefully worded position statement was difficult to disagree with. It helped diffuse anger and bolstered the faculty who appreciated the pro-academic freedom stance. Valencia's trustees exhibited tremendous leadership in adopting the position statement early, and in spite of any private reservations they may have had, holding to it throughout the run of the exhibit.

We identified the art gallery curator, art department chairman, and public relations director as the principal spokespersons. This decision protected the president from direct criticism. The position statement was distributed to reporters and using language from it, a letter was drafted to respond to angry letters. We then developed a plan to counteract negative publicity and the escalation of misinformation. We called key constituencies and alleviated their concerns. We released a letter to the media from a Catholic priest who had praised the exhibit for its compassion.

No college enjoys a controversy played out on the front pages of the newspaper and in front of a camera. But there was a positive side. More than 2000 people visited Valencia's art gallery during the showing, compared to the usual 200. Faculty was very supportive of the president, who was hailed as an academic leader among educators throughout the state.

by Lucy Boudet-Clary
Coordinator, Communications and Marketing
Valencia Community College
Orlando, Florida

Surviving a Student Death

Perhaps no event is more threatening within a college than the sudden death of a student. In October 1988, Walla Walla Community College experienced such an event for the first and only time in its history. It was with a sense of horror that administrators learned a student had been shot in a campus parking lot. The police and an ambulance were called immediately, but before any action could be taken, the assailant had shot himself as well.

Nursing faculty were summoned; they determined the unknown assailant was mortally wounded and began administering CPR to the injured female student. With the arrival of authorities, the victims were taken to the hospital, and police began to interrogate witnesses.

Once the emergency situation was over, administrators met immediately to plan how the college would handle communication during the crisis. The administrative team decided that the best interests of the victim's family, the students and the college would be served by being proactive, accurate and thorough. The president acted as the official college spokesman and the switchboard was alerted to direct all calls about the incident to the president's office. The college relations officer prepared a standby statement, confirming only the time and place of attack, the fact that the victim was a student, that the unknown assailant had shot himself, and the hospitals to which they had been taken. No names or other details were released; even in non-crisis situations, students' privacy is strictly protected by state law and by college policy.

When the hospital informed him that the student had died, the president went to the hospital to comfort the victim's family.

One of the college's chief concerns was the well-being of

faculty, staff and students. While a memorandum was issued providing an accurate account of the shooting and advising them not to make statements to reporters and asking that they direct all inquiries to the president's office, arrangements were made with counselors to work with students in the victim's program of study and with others who knew her. Upon a request by students to hold an on-campus memorial service, a non-religious service was held.

The local media were kept informed of details the college could legally issue; for information beyond the institution's dominion, they were referred to local authorities. When a local reporter requested an interview with students during one of the counseling sessions, students decided it was acceptable providing no photos were taken of their faces and no names were used. The college relations officer monitored the questioning and was prepared to stop the interview should class members become disturbed.

There appeared to be no negative consequences to the college's reputation as a result of this event. This may have been because of the proactive, caring attitude of the administration and because some basic processes were followed:

- select one spokesperson
- verify and confirm all facts immediately
- determine in advance exactly what the press will be told and be forthright in making statements
- protect students, faculty and staff from press intrusions
- act forthrightly and sincerely in working with all the parties involved
- emphasize positive aspects of the most negative event: in this case, the college's quick response, the counseling provided to distressed students, the memorial service to channel the feelings of grief.

by Peter Wilkinson
Director of College Relations
Walla Walla Community College

CHAPTER 6

Institutional Distinctiveness

by Dr. George Boggs
Superintendent/President
Palomar College

About the Author

Dr. George Boggs

 George Boggs is Superintendent/President of Palomar College in San Marcos, California. He has served as a faculty member and administrator in community colleges for twenty-five years. Dr. Boggs is an active author and presenter and is currently serving as chair-elect of the Board of Directors of the American Association of Community Colleges.

*E*ducational programs in community colleges have evolved from the limited junior college function envisioned by the founders of the movement to a comprehensive set of programs designed to meet the needs of a diverse group of students in the communities served by the colleges.   Over the years, community colleges have taken on vocational programs, remedial and developmental programs, citizenship and ESL courses, community education courses, and adult education courses.

The growth years of the 1960s and 1970s saw the colleges' missions expand to take on many new educational functions. Proposals for new programs were often acted upon quickly, and resources were allocated to these ever-expanding institutions. The community colleges developed a reputation for being extremely responsive to the needs of their communities. They fostered their image as the "people's colleges," close to the people they served.

However, as resources became less available, or as control of the colleges shifted in some parts of the country away from the communities they served to a more centralized or state governance system, the colleges were criticized for "trying to be all things to all people." The colleges then began to suffer from their lack of a well focused or clearly defined mission. Limited resources and a growing competition for students forced many of the colleges to reexamine their missions and engage in strategic planning for their futures.   Cooperative agreements were forged with nearby colleges to avoid duplication of expensive programs. Community colleges also began to develop partnerships with businesses and industries in their service areas to provide mutual support. The quest for institutional distinctiveness has become the new pattern for many community colleges.

Institutional Distinctiveness

The community colleges which are most successful are those

which have developed a well-defined mission and a shared vision of the future. The mission is a statement of the direction of an institution; it defines a clear purpose for being. The vision is a picture of what the institution will be at some point in the future. It should emerge from an understanding of the needs of the communities served by the college and of the internal strengths and abilities of the institution.

In 1988, the American Association of Community and Junior Colleges issued its vision statement for the nation's community colleges, *Building Communities, A Vision For A New Century* (AACC, 1988). This publication, a report of the Commission on the Future of Community Colleges, is really a combined vision statement for the nation's community colleges. The central theme of the report is that community colleges should build communities. The Commission defined "community" not only as a region to be served, but also as a climate to be created. Building community, the report says, must begin at home. Trustees, faculty, administrators, and students must be inspired by a shared vision for their college community.

Strategic Planning

Colleges which have developed shared visions and revised mission statements have engaged in strategic planning processes. To be most effective, these processes must involve a broad spectrum of people, including faculty and staff members, administrators, students, trustees, and community leaders. The final product must be endorsed by all segments of the college community.

A critical first step in planning is to assess the college's environment and to develop a set of assumptions about the environment in the future. This process involves gathering data from several sources: local, county, state and national governments; public schools; local businesses; other providers of higher education in the area; and local planning agencies. Essential information includes population projections and the special needs of that population (e.g., Will the new population need English language or citizenship skills? Will there be more single parent households? What will be

the age and ethnic mix of the population served by the college?).
Information needs also include planned changes in transportation
arteries, skills needed by local business and industry, future state
and local funding formulas, and the plans of other colleges or
universities in the area if they are available.

Next, the planning group should critically assess the college's
strengths and weaknesses. What does the college do well? Is the
financial condition of the college sound? Does the institution foster
a climate which encourages risk taking and innovation? What can
the college do better? Does the diversity of the faculty and staff
reflect that of the student body and the community? Are graduates
successful?

A study and comparison of the environmental planning assumptions and the strengths and weaknesses of the college are essential
as the college develops its vision for the future, a revised or reaf-
firmed mission statement, and a strategic plan. College programs
should serve the educational needs of its students and should fit the
needs of the community. The plan should take advantage of
college strengths and deal proactively with addressing weaknesses.
The educational plan should determine the staff, fiscal, facilities,
and student services plans. As these plans are implemented, the
college will carve out its own distinctive niche. It will be able to
take advantage of future opportunities and avoid the mistake of
operating without a clear and commonly understood focus.

Once the vision of a college is communicated, understood and
accepted, it must be continually reinforced and communicated.
New members of the faculty, staff, and board of trustees must be
properly oriented to the college, its mission, and its vision. Decisions must be made in accordance with the accepted plans and
values, and the college image must be shaped with the vision
statement and mission in mind.

Assessing Practices

In order to assess the degree to which strategic planning is used by
community colleges to focus their mission and to establish a vision
for the future, selected colleges were surveyed in December of

1992. This qualitative study revealed some of the ways community colleges have become distinctive and have developed and shaped their images.

Colleges selected for inclusion in the study were Beacon Colleges identified by the staff of the American Association of Community Colleges. Additional colleges were chosen on the basis of their having achieved recognition for the distinctive images they projected. An informant at each college was interviewed by telephone and asked a series of open-ended questions relating to the process by which the college defined its vision and to the impact of the image on the college. Informants were identified by contacting the office of the president on each campus, describing the study, and asking which person on campus was most likely to have the necessary information. Informants held a number of positions, including president, director of planning and research, and public information director.

Defining the Image

Responses revealed that the image of a college may result from one or more of a number of factors, including its history and location, the needs of the surrounding community, an exhaustive planning process, and the vision of the president.

Most of the colleges contacted had a mission or vision state-ment developed within the last ten years. Several were in the process of revising or updating an earlier statement. As one infor-mant put it, planning and defining an image are part of an ongoing "fluid process" in which the vision is constantly being studied and revised to ensure that it meets the needs of the college's constitu-ents.

Several of the colleges had embarked on a planning process in response to the findings of an accreditation team and did not sound as if they had undertaken the effort with much enthusiasm. How-ever, once the process was completed, they seemed to see the advantages of having gone through it. Some respondents were able to state very clearly the vision of their college and the way they wanted to be perceived. Others could not articulate the vision so explicitly, although a picture generally emerged during the course of the interview.

All of the respondents were asked to describe the image of the college that they would like to project. Considering that the colleges contacted were reputed to have created unique images, some of the responses initially seemed surprisingly conventional. Frequent references to "responsiveness" appeared to reflect the traditional community college emphasis on flexibility in adapting programs to meet emerging community needs. However, this desire to be responsive, tempered by such factors as history, geographic location, composition of the population, and characteristics of the college's leadership, produced a fascinating array of institutions that prided themselves on the unique programs for which they were noted.

A college near the Mexican border emphasized international business, another took pride in the high-quality instruction that had historically attracted a large percentage of local high school graduates, and several in multi-cultural communities emphasized diversity. Still others had built reputations for attributes said to be important to their presidents, such as "caring" or "institutional effectiveness." A respondent whose college was noted for being innovative felt this was in part due to its being a new institution that was not tied to "tried and true ways" of doing things and was therefore uniquely free to experiment.

That colleges recognize the importance of marketing is reflected in their frequent use of terms such as "customer focused" and "customer driven" to describe their method of deciding on the image they want to project. Several reported having conducted surveys in their local communities or convening focus groups to discuss community needs and the way consumers perceive their college.

Although informants outside a college might attribute its institutional uniqueness to externally funded programs, representatives of the college itself saw the image as being created from within. The insiders said that their institutions attracted external support because it was consistent with an already-agreed-upon image, rather than a determinant of that image.

While colleges may strive to project an overall image, nearly all respondents said that the way a college is perceived depends to a great extent upon who is asked about it. Business leaders may see it not as an educational institution but as a center for economic development. Senior citizens may see it as a source of reasonably priced opportunities to enjoy music, drama, dance, and art. Several respondents said they believed most people thought of their college in terms of the outstanding physical facilities that were available for use by local high school teams, arts groups, and members of the community. One college capitalized on its small size to market itself, focusing on its small classes and ready access to computers and support services.

While a college's image is usually thought of as being shaped over time, news stories can often have a dramatic and immediate effect. In an unfortunate example of the effect of negative publicity, an informant at a college that had historically had a very positive image in its community said the first thing people thought about when they heard the college's name was a recent serious financial problem.

Presidential Leadership

Informants often cited the leadership of the president as a driving factor in determining how the college is viewed in the community. One leader was described as being "entrepreneurial" and quick to see opportunities and to take advantage of them. This president encouraged environmental scanning to enable the college to identify changes in the student body and in the community and insisted that faculty and staff shift their focus from internal disagreements to the changing nature of the population they served.

On another campus, additional impetus was given to projecting the college's image because it was consistent with the president's disciplinary interests. At a college that started as a trade school, the image was in transition, with older residents perceiving it in its former job-related role, while the younger ones saw it more as the comprehensive institution it was becoming.

Rewards of a Strong Image

Success in creating a strong image has its advantages according to the informants. One college that wanted to be seen as caring and undaunted by limitations was able to face a state budget crisis by declaring it an opportunity to reinvent the college while preserving employment for full-time staff.

A college that emphasized institutional effectiveness made better decisions as collection of data about important issues replaced "seat-of-the-pants" decisionmaking. The recognition that accompanies a distinctive image helps with recruiting faculty, staff, and students. Known as an economic development resource for its community, another college benefited from technical transfer from the industries with which it worked. Its local industries contribute to the growth of the college because they believe it will help them in return. These satisfied consumers created a multiplier effect, enabling the college to reach more and different markets. The number of students in its customized training programs grew from 500 to 6,000 over a five-year period.

Sometimes one particularly strong program can shape a college's image. A college with a strong honors program attracted a high percentage of local high school graduates in an area where community colleges in general are not taken seriously.

Not Without Pain

Having a distinctive image is, as one planner said, "not without pain." Even when the college succeeds in communicating the image upon which it has decided, there may be internal conflicts precipitated by faculty or staff who disagree. Some colleges that were proud of their reputations for innovation and responsiveness to their constituencies had to deal with faculty who felt they were being left out of the governance process when courses were developed and offered quickly. They were concerned about lack of assurances in the quality of course content and delivery. At another college, a focus on international education led to objections from the local media and citizens who felt that it was not an appropriate role for a local community college. A college that emphasized empowering staff encountered opposition from those who felt the decentralized decision-making process was "wishy-washy" and resented the amount of time required to resolve problems.

These examples point out the need for a *shared* mission and vision for the college. Even then, there will be some disagreements about directions and decisions, but the ability to ground them in a shared mission and vision should aid in their acceptance.

Some of the colleges represented in this study were also dealing with dramatic changes in the nature of their student bodies caused by demographic changes in their communities. Several colleges were engaged in efforts to have a student body that reflected the diversity of their communities. However, many informants expressed a concern that the college might become too closely associated with one particular group and thereby discourage attendance by others. Creating an image of being accessible to all students was seen as being important.

Reputation

In June of 1988, the California Community College Foundation contracted with the firm of Burson-Marsteller to develop a public relations or communications program for the colleges in that state (California Community College Foundation, 1988). One of the key findings of the study done by Burson-Marsteller is that internal representatives of the local colleges believed that their own college was well-regarded, but the reputation of the California Community College system was not as favorable. This finding can probably be generalized nationally. Community colleges in general do not have the prestige of four-year colleges and universities.

Even though we may believe our own institutions are highly regarded in our communities, the image that community colleges are "second-rate" hurts all of the colleges. Traditional measures of the quality of a college are the exclusivity of its admissions standards, the number of National Merit Scholars who are enrolled, the number of Nobel laureates on the faculty, the number of library holdings, the budget of the institution, or the number of research grants received. These measures are related to inputs and processes and not learning outcomes. They do not serve community colleges well because of their open access missions and their commitment to teaching and learning.

The image we create for our institutions must emphasize their strengths. Local colleges should gather data on the outcomes of their work. Information on the success of transfers and graduates should be highlighted. The influence of the college on the economic development of the community and the economic impact of the college itself should be made known to local businesses and the community in general. Community colleges are not four-year colleges or universities, and they should not be judged on inappropriate criteria.

Begin at Home

Whether a college is old or new, large or small, traditional or change-oriented, it can draw upon resources offered by its leadership, location, history, and constituency to create and project a distinctive image, consistent with the character of the college and its responsiveness to the needs of its unique community. Ideally, the image of a college should be shaped by the conscious choice of its people. The image, if it is to be an accurate one, should emanate from shared mission and vision statements which are developed as a conclusion to some type of planning process. It should focus on the unique strengths of the college and yet also help to reinforce the image of community colleges in general. The Commission on the Future of Community Colleges reported that building community must begin at home. So must the building of an image.

REFERENCES

American Association of Community and Junior Colleges. *Building Communities, A Vision For A New Century*. Washington, D.C.: AACC, 1988.

Burson-Marsteller. *California Community Colleges Communication Review*. Sacramento: California Community College Foundation, 1988.

Partnership Promotes Distance Learning

In January 1991, Lakeshore Technical College embarked on a new and innovative approach in providing a radiography program to serve the Lakeshore, Moraine Park and Fox Valley vocational-technical districts. Via live, interactive television transmission, classes are beamed to five hospitals. Through agreements with each of the hospitals, lab and clinical experiences are provided in their respective facilities using skilled employees as adjunct faculty.

Through cooperative scheduling with Moraine Park Technical College, Fox Valley Technical College and Lakeshore Technical College, students can take general education and other supporting technical classes at a local technical college and remain in their respective communities. The technology that is being used to provide the radiography program may serve as a prototype to expand educational opportunities in educational programs throughout the nation and provide a new concept in sharing between groups of technical colleges and employers.

In fall 1992, an accreditation visitation committee of the Joint Review Committee and Radiologic Technology commended the radiography program for its "innovative approach to delivery of education."

The team listed the major strengths of the radiography program as: 1) innovative approach to delivery of education, supported by Lakeshore Technical College, other districts and the health care community, 2) radiography administrators and staff who play an active role in the delivery of education to students, 3) continual monitoring of presentation materials via television to increase program effectiveness, and 4) individuals at the college and the clinic sites who embrace change.

by Dick Romaine
Public Information/Communications Specialist
Lakeshore Technical College
Cleveland, Wisconsin

Guaranteeing Your Product

In September 1989, Northeast Community College formed a Marketing Committee of 21 members, representing a cross-section of the campus community. One of the seven subcommittees was charged with looking into college image.

While gathering its research, the image committee discovered an article on a state college which had developed a written job guarantee for graduates of their teachers college. Not only did the college guarantee its graduates a teaching job somewhere in the U.S., it also guaranteed school districts employing their graduates that they would be satisfactory first-year teachers. The article also carried information about other institutions offering competency guarantees.

As a result of the article, committee members contacted several two- and four-year colleges which had tried educational guarantees. The overwhelmingly positive response convinced members that developing competency guarantees would effectively improve educational quality and college image at the same time.

These findings were presented to the college president along with a recommendation that competency guarantees for students and employers be developed. The committee sought to reposition Northeast as the college with the written guarantees. To date six college programs have developed board-approved competency guarantees for students and employers, and several other programs are in the process.

The Marketing Committee has since become the Marketing Council, with full status as a permanent part of the college organizational structure. In June 1992, the board of governors approved the first marketing plan for Northeast Community College. Three goals serve as the backbone of the plan: enrollment, quality and image.

by Craig Kinsella
Instructor, Management and Marketing
Northeast Community College
Norfolk, Nebraska

A Student Outcomes Model That Works

Santa Fe Community College initiated a student outcomes assessment process in 1986 to evaluate and improve its educational programs. The assessment methods are relevant to student goals and the college's educational mission. The process has become a valuable tool for internal quality control, continuous program improvement, and efficient reporting to external agencies.

Specifically, the Student Outcomes Model is designed to: 1) identify what the college wants to teach, 2) measure the degree to which the college is doing it, and 3) collect information to help do it better. In reality, the SFCC outcomes studies are an ongoing series of brief, practical, issues-oriented reports with applications to specific instructional practices or programs. The studies (and subsequent reports) reflect continuous attention to program improvement and instructional enhancement. The process places student outcomes as an integral function of the college's total quality control system.

The studies, conducted annually, are simple, relevant and provide usable information. The format and procedures meet the standards of formal research to establish validity and reliability but remain simple to carry out. The simplicity encourages faculty and staff to conduct issues-oriented studies under the coordination of a college-wide Student Outcomes Committee.

Among the annual studies are:

- Correlation study: final exams and acquired competencies
- Licensure exams success rates
- Student opinion surveys
- Graduate follow-up study

- Employer follow-up study
- College transfer study
- Course success and completion rates study

Critical to the success of measuring effectiveness is a commitment to separate student outcomes assessment from staff or faculty performance evaluations. Outcomes work is most successful when faculty and staff enthusiastically seek out opportunities to participate.

Since 1986, the outcomes data also has proven useful for meeting agency reporting requirements. As a measure of institutional effectiveness, the studies have been used in the accreditation and self-study process. As a measure of academic gain, the studies are incorporated into federal vocational reporting standards. The studies are also a vital component of the consumer information made available to new and prospective students.

by Anthony Garcia, Dean of Students
Santa Fe Community College
Sante Fe, New Mexico